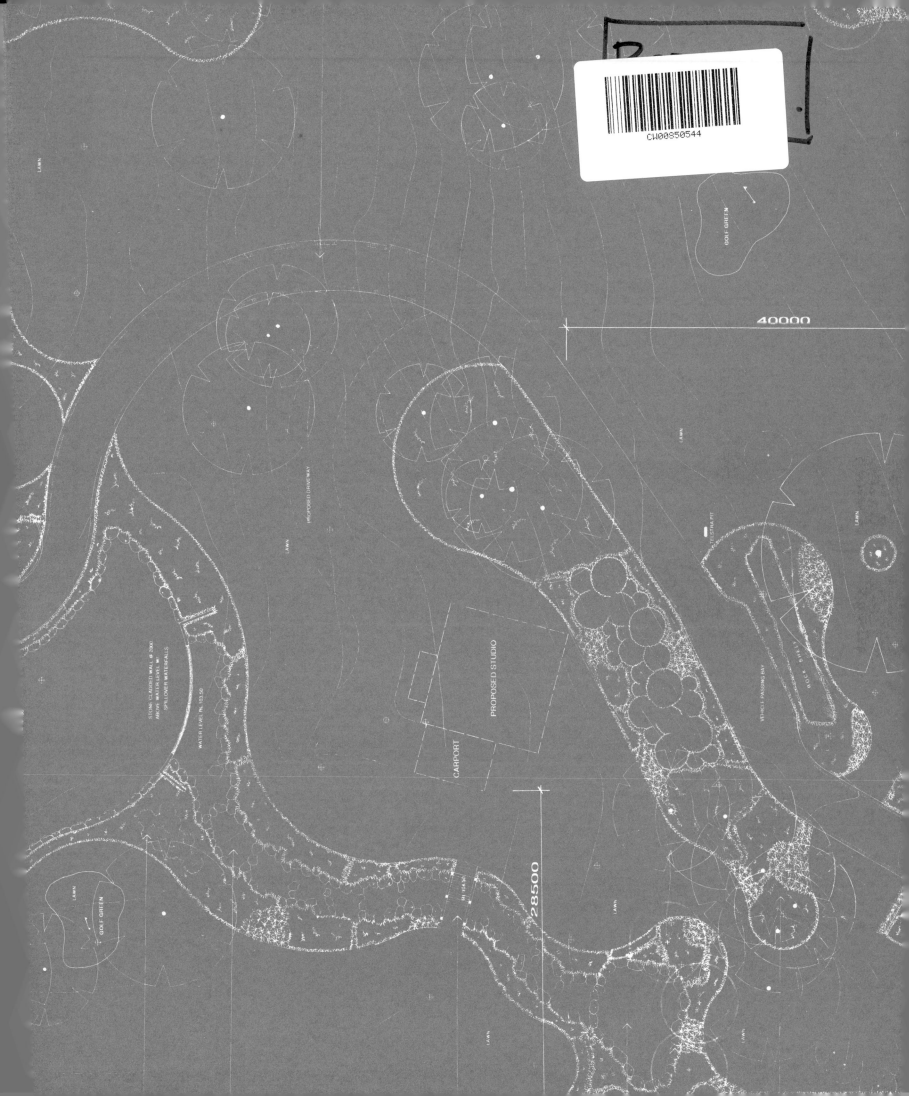

40000

28500

LAWN

GOLF GREEN

GOLF GREEN

LAWN

LAWN

LAWN

LAWN

LAWN

LAWN

LAWN

LAWN

PROPOSED DRIVEWAY

PROPOSED STUDIO

CARPORT

STONE CLADDED WALL @ 3000
ABOVE WATER LEVEL W/
SPILLOVER WATERFALLS

WATER LEVEL RL 103.50

RL 104.50

ROCK SHELF

VEHICLE PASSING BAY

TELSTRA PIT

RESORT STYLE LIVING

RESORT STYLE LIVING

JAMIE
DURIE
PUBLISHING

DEAN HERALD

PHOTOGRAPHY BY DANNY KILDARE

PUBLISHED BY JAMIE DURIE PUBLISHING

JPD MEDIA PTY LTD
ABN 83 098 894 761
35 Albany Street
Crows Nest NSW 2065
PHONE: + 61 2 9026 7444
FAX: + 61 2 9026 7475

FOUNDER AND EDITORIAL DIRECTOR: Jamie Durie
GROUP CREATIVE DIRECTOR: Nadine Bush

PUBLISHER: Nicola Hartley
DEVELOPMENTAL EDITOR: Bettina Hodgson
DESIGN CONCEPT AND ART DIRECTION: Amanda Emmerson
DESIGN: Amanda Emmerson, Criena Court and Geraldine Ward
PUBLISHING SERVICES MANAGER: Belinda Smithyman
PUBLISHING ASSISTANT AND PRODUCTION: Michelle Kavanagh
EDITOR: Susin Chow
PHOTOGRAPHY: Danny Kildare
ARCHITECTURAL DRAWINGS: Dean Herald
PROPS: Equator Homewares, Freedom Furniture, Bed Bath N' Table, Rapee,
My Island Home, Domayne, Kas Australia, Top 3 By Design, SIA Homewares
and Dedon.

DISTRIBUTED BY: HarperCollins*Publishers* Australia

National Library of Australia Cataloguing-in-Publication data:
Herald, Dean.
Resort style living.

1st ed.
Bibliography.
Includes index.
ISBN 978 0 9757361 2 8

1. Gardens - Australia - Design. 2. Landscape design -
Australia. I. Chow, Susin. II. Kildare, Danny. III.
Title.

712.0994

Set in Gotham on InDesign
Printed in Singapore by Tien Wah Press
First printed in 2007

10 9 8 7 6 5 4 3 2 1

ACKNOWLEDGEMENTS

Thank you to all of my clients who have given me the opportunity to develop
their outdoor living environments, and a special thank you to all who allowed
their properties to be featured in this book.

To my design and construction staff—your commitment and vision to each
project is shown in the quality of the finished product. A special thank you to
Matt Denton and Mark Heath for your continual commitment to excellence in
construction and management of the projects in conjunction with Cameron
Bradley, Luke Passaro, Michael Lillyman and Grant Kriss. Thank you to Justin
Dibble and James Caruso for your dedication in the design studio and your
design input into projects we work on together.

Thank you to my core group of suppliers, in particular Eco Concepts, Kastell
Kitchens, Alpine Nurseries, ME Lighting, Axolotl Ozone, Sareen Stone, Marcus
Engineering and Reliance Pools.

A special thank you to Wes Fleming and his parents Don and Dawn for the
adventure we shared in creating the Chelsea Show garden, your generosity
and vision for the industry is amazing.

Thank you to David Denton of Denton Homes for your vision in creating
prestige homes and for embracing my vision to enhance them.

Thank you to Jamie Durie for the opportunity to produce this book and the
enormous contribution you have given to the industry, which is too often
unrecognised.

A special thank you to Nicci Hartley, Bettina Hodgson, Amanda Emmerson,
Criena Court and Michelle Kavanagh from Jamie Durie Publishing for your
enthusiasm and creative direction with my work. Our dealings together have
been a complete pleasure and you have produced a book that has truly
captured my vision.

To my Mum and Dad, brother Justin and sister Sharlene, thank you for your
love and support.

Thank you to Danny Kildare—your photography has brought my work to
life and it has been captured in such a stunning way. Thank you for your
dedication to excellence with every shot taken.

And now to my amazing wife Bernice, thank you for your continuous support
and belief in me, you enable me to do what I love doing with ease, and that is
a priceless gift. To my two boys Nixon & Bryson... Dad has finally finished the
book, time to play cars.

CONTENTS

0 : Introduction 1

1 : Space 5

2 : Entertainment 41

3 : Relaxation 71

4 : Water 101

5 : Living 131

INTRODUCTION

WE ALL LOVE A BIT OF LUXURY in life and I believe this should not be excluded in the outdoor space of our homes. During the past 13 years I have enjoyed many opportunities to work closely with clients who have given me the freedom to express my interpretation of an outdoor space in line with their lifestyle needs. This privileged experience has enabled me to grow both personally and professionally, and to develop unique designs that reflect a resort style approach to living.

Resort-style living is about function, comfort and relaxation, which embraces the use of space and our relationship within it. In my childhood I lived in a number of homes that had a similar look and feel. The backyard was a mixed variety of lawn with a decent percentage of bindii, some kind of shrubby thing along the fence line and the 'feature' skinny concrete path leading to the clothes line. There was little to no shade cover, the barbecue was a steel plate sitting on a stack of leftover house bricks and the garden shed for some reason was visible from most rooms in the house. Even the architecture of those homes did not encourage interaction between the indoors and outdoors, with an enclosed floor plan and single rear door access to the garden.

By the time I was 19, I was bursting with ideas to change those types of homes. So, with my qualifications and the basic skills of landscaping under my belt, I started my own business, Rolling Stone Landscapes.

In the early years I mainly worked in new housing estates. The landscape designs were fairly basic, and the budgets low, but I took pleasure in interacting with clients and producing a garden tailored to their needs. I enjoyed the challenges of business, staff and client relationships, but as time moved on I found that I wanted to take more control of the work I produced and attract a broader clientele. I have always had a passion for hotel resorts and the emotions they evoke in us—whether we're standing in one or looking at a picture in a travel brochure. Even though at the time this style was a niche market with a limited clientele, I decided to take on the challenge of creating fully customised outdoor spaces that captured the experience of resort-style living.

At first I would sit at the drawing table all night designing resort-style pools and water features, dreaming and hoping that my clients would allow me to take my designs into the construction phase. Amazingly, they did, and this proved to me that the love of resort-style gardens was universal. The project sizes grew along with the size of the company and I started to gain a reputation for the style of design I loved.

The garden of today continues to move forward in leaps and bounds. I believe that it not only enhances the architecture of the home, it now influences the building's design. The garden has become a true extension of the home, providing a functional space for entertainment and relaxation that also evokes the senses.

This book is a collaboration of my work to date, intended to challenge and inspire the way you look at your own outdoor space. Throughout the chapters I describe the elements of resort-style design, and how these can best be integrated into your own garden to create a unique outdoor living experience that is reflective of your own needs and style.

Landscape design is many things to many people, but to me it is functional with a personal connection to those who use and view the space. We are blessed in this world with so many brilliant designers and in some way all have added their personal touch to shaping this craft. I am honoured with this opportunity to showcase my work and trust you enjoy my vision of resort-style living.

1

1

space

THERE ARE MANY ELEMENTS OF landscape design, but I have always had a passion for the designing of space and the movement within it. The correct layout of all the required elements within a garden is the strength of the design and communicates the story of the space.

Designing and building a garden is an amazing opportunity to create a personally tailored environment to suit your desired lifestyle. It is also an opportunity to investigate the vast selection of design materials available and discover the wonder of plant life. Over the years outdoor living has continued to develop, and we now have even more opportunities to extend and enhance the experience—cooking units have evolved into full outdoor kitchens, pools are more than just places to swim, and outdoor heating has lengthened the amount of time we spend in the garden throughout the seasons.

When starting a garden design, there are many factors that need contemplation and detailed investigation. Every garden has common and individual characteristics to take into account, and no two sites—or home owners—are the same. However, while the unique quality of each space will bring with it new ideas for design, there are a number of key factors that I believe are fundamental to the success of any garden design. This chapter highlights the essential considerations of garden space, including scale, aspect, function and theme.

The aspect of the property is an unchangeable factor and cannot be ignored. It will determine the selection of plants, as well as how the area can be used. Aspect will also influence the placement of structures and their design, whether for shade, screening or feature use.

The scale of the garden is another important factor to consider, as the correct scale gives the garden its natural balance to the eye. Scale will affect every design decision in the garden, especially the selection and placement of items within the space such as furnishings, plants, water features and sculptures.

The desired function of the garden is one of the most influential factors in its design; it is the underlying purpose which we sense when we first enter a designed landscape. Whether a tranquil garden setting for the morning newspaper and coffee, an intimate retreat to escape from the world or the ultimate in outdoor entertaining with pool, kitchen and sound system, function is instantly recognisable in a successful design.

Once these key factors are considered, you can begin to apply the selected theme or style of the garden. The home's architecture can play the strongest role in the selection of a garden theme, but it can be adapted in keeping with your preferred style. The theme is supported by the use of design materials, especially plants, which will continue to add strength to the design as they mature into their desired heights and purpose.

SCALE

SCALE IS AN ESSENTIAL CONSIDERATION when starting to design any outdoor space. It is the visual communication confirming if you got it right or wrong. The principles of scale apply to all elements of the garden, whether it is the size of the pool, the choice of paving material or the expected maturity of the plants. Take the time to understand the scale of the area you have and the elements you would like to have within it, combine this with the right plant selection, and you will have a space that feels welcoming and balanced.

The scale of the garden has a great impact on its intended function. This is most evident in the design of outdoor entertaining areas. One question I always ask my clients is how many people they would usually have at a casual function: this enables me to design an area that caters not only for an appropriately sized table and seating but is also correct for the scale of the space. Importantly, the space around the table should provide a comfortable clearance for traffic, as it is critical for movement around the table and to other parts of the garden.

The size of the outdoor space itself will determine the scale of any design, but the selection and placement of elements within the garden is the key to its success. When designing a garden in a large property, some elements and features will need to be larger than for a smaller property so that they will be in correct scale. This may mean that pathways are wider, entertaining areas are more spacious and even the pool is of grand proportions. Sculptures and ornamental features play an artistic role, and also provide a personal connection to the home owner; however, the size of these features also needs careful consideration to ensure that they are not too small or too large. All these elements combine to assist in giving the outdoor space its correct scale—that sense of getting it right which is felt from any part of the garden.

Plants, of course, also play a major role in complementing the designed space, and understanding the expected maturity of each plant installed is a vital part of the design process. We all have seen large trees that are clearly not appropriate for the size of the location they are growing in; as well as expanses of paved areas that are crying out for the softening touch that plant life brings. This is the result of poor design and a lack of understanding of the plants installed, and the incorrect scale gives you a negative impression of the space instead of embracing you within it.

A successfully designed garden is one that has a calculated plan for the plants' maturity, but also achieves its desired function on a daily basis. One of the most frequently requested designs is for screen planting on the boundaries of properties, especially as new homes are getting closer to each other. Understanding the scale and desired maturity of screen planting, as well as the garden's aspect and climate, will enable you to shorten the list of the available plant species for screening so you are only left with the choice of colour and texture to consider. With the correct soil preparation, drainage and watering, there will be little reason why those plants will not achieve their intended maturity, along with a healthy appearance that complements the space in the meantime.

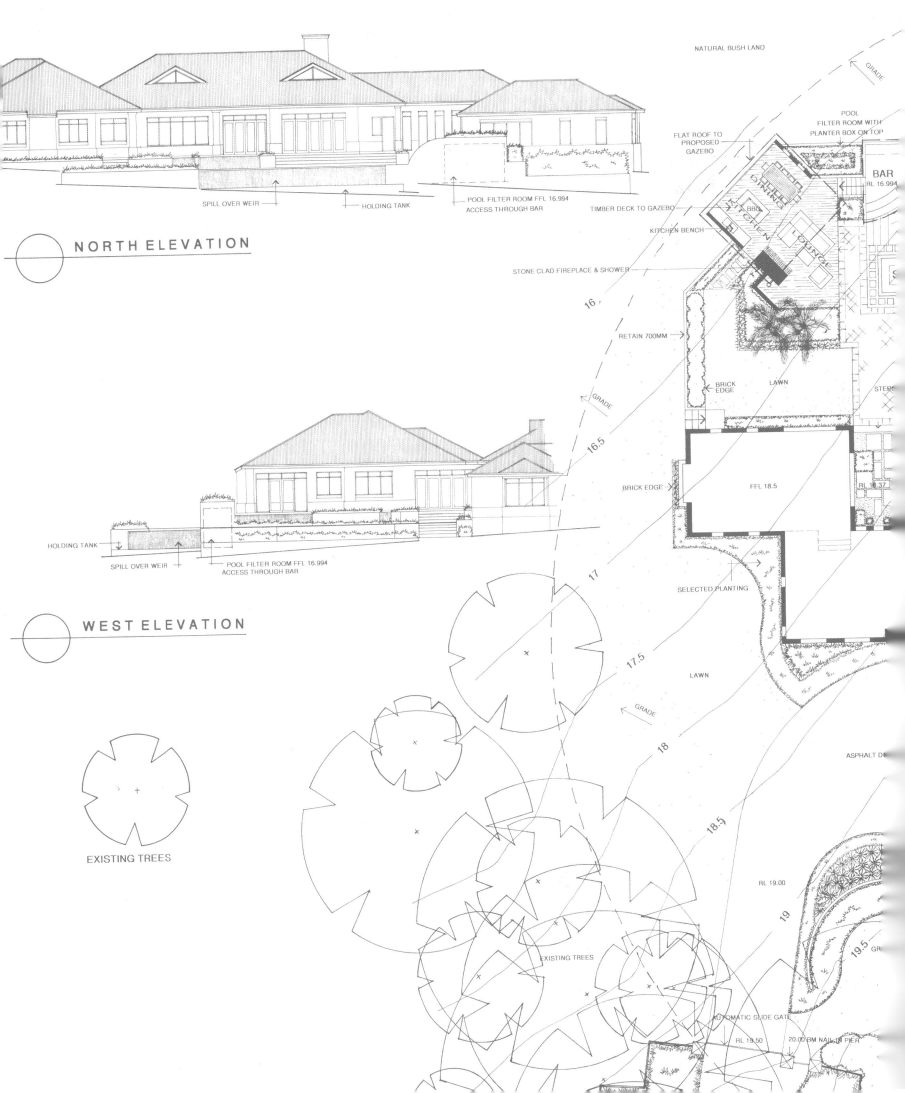

NORTH ELEVATION

SPILL OVER WEIR   HOLDING TANK   POOL FILTER ROOM FFL 16.994
ACCESS THROUGH BAR

WEST ELEVATION

HOLDING TANK

SPILL OVER WEIR   POOL FILTER ROOM FFL 16.994
ACCESS THROUGH BAR

EXISTING TREES

NATURAL BUSH LAND

GRADE

POOL
FILTER ROOM WITH
PLANTER BOX ON TOP

FLAT ROOF TO
PROPOSED
GAZEBO

BAR
RL 16.994

TIMBER DECK TO GAZEBO

KITCHEN BENCH

KITCHEN   BBQ   DINING   LOUNGE

STONE CLAD FIREPLACE & SHOWER

RETAIN 700MM

BRICK
EDGE   LAWN

STERS

BRICK EDGE   FFL 18.5   RL 18.37

16

GRADE

16.5

SELECTED PLANTING

17

LAWN

17.5

GRADE

18

ASPHALT D

18.5

RL 19.00

19

EXISTING TREES

19.5   GR

AUTOMATIC SLIDE GATE

RL 19.50   20.00 BM NAIL IN PIER

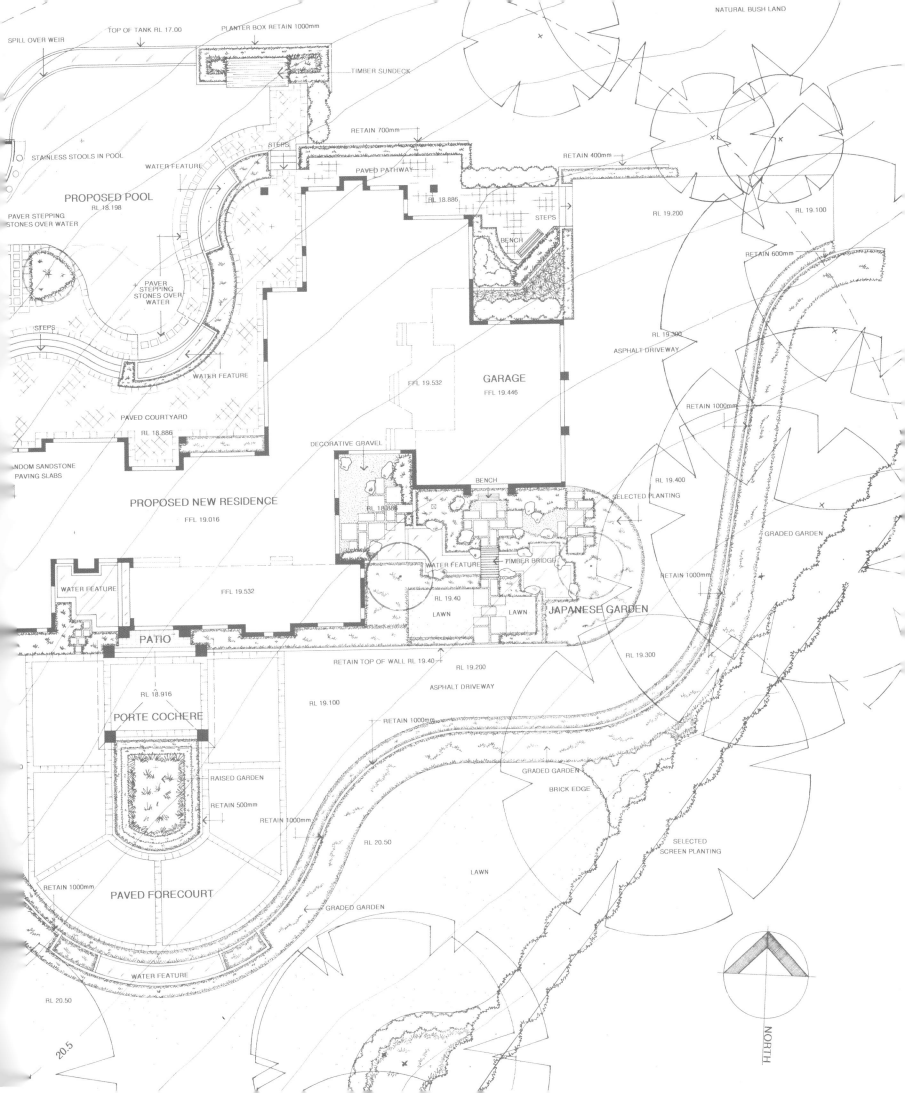

NATURAL BUSH LAND

TOP OF TANK RL 17.00   PLANTER BOX RETAIN 1000mm

SPILL OVER WEIR

TIMBER SUNDECK

RETAIN 700mm

RETAIN 400mm

STEPS

RL 18.886

PAVED PATHWAY

WATER FEATURE

RL 19.200   RL 19.100

PROPOSED POOL
RL 18.198

STAINLESS STOOLS IN POOL

STEPS

BENCH

RETAIN 600mm

PAVER STEPPING
STONES OVER WATER

PAVER
STEPPING
STONES OVER
WATER

RL 19.300

ASPHALT DRIVEWAY

STEPS

WATER FEATURE

FFL 19.532

GARAGE

FFL 19.446

RETAIN 1000mm

PAVED COURTYARD

RL 18.886

DECORATIVE GRAVEL

RL 19.400

RANDOM SANDSTONE
PAVING SLABS

BENCH

RL 18.886

SELECTED PLANTING

PROPOSED NEW RESIDENCE

FFL 19.016

GRADED GARDEN

WATER FEATURE

TIMBER BRIDGE

RL 19.40

RETAIN 1000mm

WATER FEATURE

FFL 19.532

LAWN   LAWN

JAPANESE GARDEN

PATIO

RETAIN TOP OF WALL RL 19.40   RL 19.200

RL 19.300

RL 18.916

ASPHALT DRIVEWAY

PORTE COCHERE

RL 19.100

RETAIN 1000mm

RAISED GARDEN

GRADED GARDEN

RETAIN 500mm

BRICK EDGE

RETAIN 1000mm

RETAIN 1000mm

RL 20.50

SELECTED
SCREEN PLANTING

PAVED FORECOURT

LAWN

GRADED GARDEN

WATER FEATURE

RL 20.50

20.5

NORTH

ASPECT

ALL GARDENS RELY ON CORRECT planning for the long-term sustainability of their future. This means understanding the garden's aspect—its relationship to the elements, how the sun moves over the property, and the effects of other weather conditions such as wind or rain. The aspect of an existing property cannot be changed, but if ignored it can result in the failure of the design within a short period of time. The outdoor elements are to be respected and used to your advantage to ensure the success of the garden.

Working with the four seasons brings exciting opportunities to highlight different features of a garden design during the year. For example, in a flowering garden design, plants can be selected to display colour throughout the seasons and not only in spring and summer. Deciduous plants can be a very powerful tool in a garden's design, providing protection from the sun during the hotter months while allowing the warmth of the winter sun to reach us when required. During these seasonal changes, many of these plants display brilliant autumn foliage colour, adding another dimension to the garden. And once the foliage has fully dropped, we can enjoy the structural beauty of the trees' trunks and branches—again, a different feature of the garden design.

As the seasons change, the height of the sun will vary and so will the amount of sunlight in the garden. This can turn areas which received full sun in summer into shaded aspects, or the sun may reach areas that previously had less direct light. This can be comforting in winter, allowing the warmth of the winter sun to reach sitting areas or provide filtered light between trees. The sun's movements over the garden will also give each area a different look and feel, and these have a relationship to the time of the day. The morning light is gentle and soft as it highlights the tips of the foliage. The midday sun brings a total covering of light to most areas, providing a true indication of the actual colours of pool designs and other surrounding structures. As the afternoon sets in, the sun casts long shadows that form interesting shapes over the garden, while other areas glow with the rays of sunset falling upon them.

The variety of aspects that is found in a garden provides the opportunity to introduce a wide planting palette, from full sun through to full shade if the property allows. A large proportion of plants do prefer full sun, but plants need to be selected for what they will achieve and not for how good they look in the garden centre. There is also a great variety of shade-loving plants with stunning features and while these aren't always suitable for all gardens, in those with a shaded aspect they can create a spectacular display. Generally you will find that plants in shade have a slower growth rate, but this should not affect your selection.

Most gardens will also have negative aspects, such as strong winds or scorching sun, but plant material can be used to reduce the effects of these. Large screening plants can reduce the harshness of the western sun in summer, or provide a windbreak for a location that is effected by gales and prevailing winds. If strong winds are a factor, garden structures will also assist in deflecting them away from specific areas. Shaded aspects can be created with the installation of trees, if spaces allows; this introduces a microclimate, where the canopy of trees protects the underplanting beneath it.

FUNCTION

THE SUCCESS OF ANY WELL-DESIGNED landscape is proven when you don't actually notice the design at all. By this I mean that if an outdoor space has been designed with functionality in mind, you will move through the space and interact with it effortlessly. So while a well-designed landscape is a combination of many elements, in my opinion, the way it meets its purpose—its function—is the most important.

Over the years of designing hundreds of gardens, I have found that the most crucial part of the process is spending time with the client to gain a true understanding of how they intend to use the outdoor space, as well as learning about their lifestyle, family and friends. As mentioned previously, one of the first questions I ask is how many friends and family they would usually have at a casual function such as a barbecue. This is of critical importance in designing the paved areas for outdoor dining, and cooking if required, and from there we can start to consider furniture layouts. Once these basic considerations are determined, we can access the remaining space and elements within it, and start to introduce levels of innovation to build on a selected theme and style.

With my love of architecture, I am often inspired by the design of homes and buildings, and in particular their internal layouts. Over the years I have continued to push what are commonly known as 'interior elements' into the outdoor environment. The barbecue on a trolley has evolved into a full outdoor kitchen, with all the inclusions normally found in an indoor kitchen: large glass-door fridges providing inviting views of your favourite drinks; cooking units and bench space for preparing and serving food; and deep sinks with hot and cold running water. The inclusion of dishwashers and microwaves is also becoming more common.

All of these elements help to ensure that the space is tailored to meet the desired function, providing true enjoyment of outdoor entertaining with little effort.

The garden is a common destination for relaxation, but it is easier to relax if the space is designed for that function and the surrounding environment is supportive of its purpose. When planning a garden, areas can be developed to assist and increase the relaxing experience. Relaxation should be expressed in the layout of the space, with a natural view or a created one, the tranquil movement of water or the seclusion of overhanging trees. Features and elements within the space should also encourage relaxation: for example, the look and style of furniture should entice you to put your feet up or recline for a quick nap.

Plant material is a vital element when considering the function of an outdoor space. Plants provide living statements, soften edges, and support and build on the garden's theme. They can also screen neighbouring properties and provide shade or shelter to selected areas. The inclusion of fragrant plants can embrace the look and feel of the space, but it can also provide a natural perfume throughout the garden and home.

All gardens should be designed for some level of use; however, an outdoor space that reflects resort-style living has a broad range of functions. One of the most important is the use of the pool, perhaps with a relaxing spa nearby and other features that invite interaction with the water. You can even further enhance the resort-style environment with the inclusion of a swim-up bar— just as you would find at a luxurious hotel. Places to play, such as a tennis court or playground, are also important functions of outdoor spaces that reflect the resort-style living experience.

VIEW

THE VIEW OF A GARDEN FROM INSIDE the home can be just as powerful as when you are within it. It can produce a variety of feelings depending on the time of day and the current season. It can inspire, provide comfort or be tranquil. It can confirm if it's raining as you watch the raindrops form perfect circles in a pond or pool nearby. The visual impact of a garden should firstly impress and communicate to you, and secondly it should tempt you to draw you into its space. It removes you from within the four walls of the home and takes you into a less restricted environment that is continuously changing with the light and the seasons.

Inside, the view of the garden can reinforce a theme, style or mood that is in keeping with the architecture of the home, and it can also bring a sense of space to small rooms while providing additional natural light. The use of the rooms within the home generally influences the use of the areas outside them, and continuing the function of internal rooms into the garden supports the design of both. Living rooms open to outdoor living areas, kitchens connect to dining areas outside, while the view from a bedroom or study may be more tranquil or reflect a greater natural environment.

One of the most important views to consider is the front of the property. The design of front-entry gardens should clearly indicate the correct direction to the main entry of the home, and their style is usually determined by the architecture of the house and other buildings. Whether the design is open and allows a full view of the home and front door, or is more adventurous with overhanging plantings and winding pathways that surprise you at every turn, front gardens play a major role in the view for those who visit your property and direct them to and from the home.

Modern home design has embraced open-plan living and quite often this is evident from the moment you open the front door. In most open-plan designs, from the front door you have a clear view of the internal layout and finishes of the home, but your vision is also drawn through the space to the back of the property where the garden, with its water movement and plant life, welcomes you. This brings amazing opportunities to the design potential of a property.

For properties that are blessed with a view of water or a natural landscape, the placement of outdoor entertaining and relaxation areas should always take advantage of these elements. It is important to ensure the long-term growth of the garden will not obstruct your vision, and you can afford to relax the focal elements within the garden's design so that they complement, not compete with, the borrowed view. For example, in a coastal property, the ocean is a perfect backdrop for a pool design where the edges of each vanish and the two bodies of water are brought together; in this case, a simplistic paving design and planting scheme is all that is required to complement the view and bring it into the home. Similar considerations are made when dealing with a view of a natural landscape; the placement of structures and planting and material selection should not distract from the scene, letting nature take its rightful place in the design.

22

DIRECTION

THE FLOW OF MOVEMENT WITHIN a garden can be one of its most powerful elements and requires close consideration when designing its layout. The garden has to communicate with those who enter it, giving directions for its use and for travel to and from selected areas. When within a well-designed garden, you are led into its many areas without being aware of it.

Focal points within the garden act as signage boards for direction. When placed in the correct locations they ensure that you are drawn to every feature of the designed space, especially those you might not have noticed otherwise. They can be used to direct movement through the garden from one part to another, or as a final marker in a special location. However, in small gardens with the total area in view, multiple focal points should be avoided as they compete with the overall vision; it is best to select one strong focal point and let it take its place.

Focal points can be many things and will be influenced by the design and style of the garden as well as personal choice. I love the use of sculpture pieces to draw the eye and movement, and to bring a personal touch to the space. Running water is a gentle form of communication and can be used in so many ways. A free-standing water feature always draws attention through sight and sound, leading you towards it. Water features designed like natural creeks with running water close to the ground or flowing down from one point to a lower one encourage you to follow them.

Plants have one of the strongest roles in directing the flow of the garden. With the almost endless varieties available, plants provide the opportunity to direct movement and tell the garden's story. Group plantings, especially in rows, support the directional concept that is often found in the design of structural elements such as buildings, but can be just as effective when set within a lawn or in more natural surrounds.

The use of changing levels within the garden is not only practical on some sites, but also provides further opportunities to create and reinforce direction within the garden. We are naturally drawn to explore and the installation of steps and pathways throughout the garden assists in leading us through it.

If room allows, the installation of an arbour pathway makes a dramatic statement in the garden, but also acts like a corridor and gives clear direction. Even a small arbour placed correctly can create a doorway effect that draws your attention. Arbours also provide a platform for climbing plants which twist in and out of the structure and display foliage, flowers and colour throughout the seasons.

The pattern of the paving is a very strong definition of an area and it also directs movement to and from garden locations. Pavers now come in a variety of shapes, sizes and colours, which creates many options in garden design. Stretcher bond or brick pattern is one of the strongest directional paving patterns you can install; the lines are easy to visualise and if using the smaller pavers, curves can be made with little or no cutting to distract your attention. Changing the paving—whether it's paver size, colour or laying pattern—as you enter into an entertaining area or relaxation zone can communicate the intention of that designed space. This can also be used to draw attention to another part of the garden if you choose. Other materials can also be used in paving to assist in communicating direction. For example, inlaid patterns and hand-placed pebble inlays are not only decorative design features, they also play a role in directing movement.

SMALL SPACES

THE SIZE OF AN OUTDOOR SPACE doesn't prevent the design from expressing resort-style living. This garden style is about function, relaxation and convenience, which can be achieved whether in a courtyard area, an urban garden or rural property. With careful consideration to its design, a small garden can adopt elements that are tailored to its function and the enjoyment of resort-style living and, using the right material, it can also appear larger than it actually is.

For smaller outdoor spaces, the issue of scale is crucial. These locations can be designed to include many elements and still give the illusion of space. However, the scale and selection of materials needs to assist in this illusion. For example, large format pavers will reduce the number of joints visible, and the use of decking can make a space appear longer. I have often utilised a 45-degree layout for timber decking, stretching from corner to corner, which creates an even greater illusion of distance than a front-to-back layout and also allows more scope for placement of features and plants.

The design of these smaller spaces generally needs to be more innovative than for larger gardens. It will be common for areas to be integrated more closely, whether dining and cooking, or entertaining area and poolside paving. As well as multi-purpose areas, small gardens should aim to include elements with multiple uses. Custom-built bench seating incorporated into the design provides permanent seating while not intruding on the space. Bench seating takes up less space than chairs, and can also be designed to double as storage boxes for pool toys, cushions and other items used in the area. Water features in smaller gardens can also assist in space saving, such as water running down a wall, while still allowing the gentle sound of water movement to be heard.

When considering the planting for these areas, the size and growth habit of the plants are very important factors. With a limited area you cannot afford for a plant to grow in a manner that will affect the usable space or exceed its desired size. The movements of the sun, as well as the heat that can radiate from surrounding walls and buildings, should also be considered when choosing plant material. The selection of plant species will need to be suited to the garden's conditions and aspect, as well as complement the preferred look and style of the design.

Within these smaller outdoor spaces, the use of potted plants can work well. This allows the softening of plant material to be introduced without the bulk and scale that a garden bed can have. While the watering of plants in pots needs to be considered as they are often forgotten and will dry out much faster than plants set within the ground, the use of pots is a valuable opportunity to introduce an additional layer of furnishings to the design, with personal selections of colour, texture, shape and form.

EXPANSIVE SPACES

MANY GARDENS ARE BLESSED WITH wide open spaces or large parcels of land, and this can be extremely rewarding in landscape design as the limitations and boundaries of space are often removed. The expansiveness of these locations makes available many opportunities for expression of style and exploration of themed areas.

With the space available on large properties, there's an enormous range of features that can be included to enhance the experience and enjoyment of the garden. Water features, for example, are used not only as focal points of the design but can actually be the life source of the garden. The contours of the property can be manipulated to collect and store water, allowing it to be distributed when required. These waterscapes also provide a location for bird life and other native animals to call home. More than just an ornamental feature, the presence of water in the garden forms an ecosystem.

The use of lawn in expansive gardens mirrors the openness of the landscape, and also plays a part in connecting different areas together. The availability of ground space and its variations provides the opportunity to tease out the levels with rolls and falls of lawn which add interest to what would normally be a flat area.

The selection of plant material that can be used in large gardens is often greater than for smaller spaces, especially when it comes to trees. Where space is restricted, such as in a courtyard or suburban garden, grand trees can't be considered within the planting schedule. The acreage landscape, however, provides the necessary space for these beautiful trees to grow and to make a horticultural statement, whether avenue planting or within broad lawn areas.

In a large garden there is great potential to create themed areas as well as develop the main style of the design. There will be many aspects to work with, allowing you to change themes by introducing suitable materials, plants and layout. Feature elements and focal points can be placed to encourage exploration, while pathways can add a sense of mystery and adventure as they lead to secret gardens, outstanding views or entertaining areas. It is important, however, that the style and scale of features installed complement the location, and that the natural balance between hard structures and soft is retained, to enable the design to convey its message.

One of the most valuable assets of a large garden is the ability to make an entrance. The entry is your first impression of the property. It is a statement that also reflects what lies within. The driveway design plays a most important role here, leading guests from the entry and in a direction that winds through the landscape to unveil the home in its location. The movement and storage of vehicles is critical to the success of the property's design: not only does it have to be practical in its function and location, but it should also be discrete in appearance and in scale with the surroundings. The surface material of the driveway and the planting around it will also need to be considered, to ensure that they enhance the overall experience of entering the property.

THEME

THEMED GARDENS ARE DESIGNED to represent, reflect or suggest a recognisable style, origin or cultural inspiration. Culture, in conjunction with the architecture of the time, has played an invaluable role in the evolution of garden design for thousands of years. A themed garden is a great opportunity to introduce a personal style, whether for the entire garden or a dedicated space within the garden. Themes provide the perfect opportunity to introduce elements of design, complementary materials and a wide choice of plant life. When a themed garden is designed and installed correctly, it is an asset that brings rewarding benefits to those who use it and is an enticing vision from the home.

When designing a themed garden, there are many elements to consider. Firstly, you need to decide how strong you want the theme to appear. For example, most of us immediately recognise a traditional-style Japanese garden when we see one, but the more subtle elements of this theme can be adopted to suggest a Japanese influence without the theme dominating the vision of the garden. This could include the use of some of the structural elements such as circular openings, traditional pebble coverings, or a selection of classical Japanese plant species such as Japanese maples (*Acer palmatum*) and bamboo.

If you prefer to represent a traditional theme, you will need to consider elements that are true to its origin to ensure the success of the design. The layout and aspect of the garden are crucial considerations, especially if the theme requires a certain amount of sunlight or shade, or includes a particular planting style. The structural elements may require traditional installation methods and the material used will need to be as authentic as possible.

The planting is of immense importance in a themed garden, lifting the design to its intended impression. It is vital to investigate the planting requirements of the theme, and choose those plants that are suited to your garden's climate so that their future growth will continue to support the design. This may require research and sourcing of the selected plant stock, and possibly special soil preparation to warrant their survival. Most plants in a theme or style can be substituted by others that are more suitable for your location, but this will require detailed research to ensure the desired outcome is achieved.

In themed gardens, traditional or informal, the furnishings will enable the design to communicate its intended message. The placement of these items—whether seating, pots, statues or water features—is critical to the design and careful consideration should be given to this. They should appear to take their place within the garden as if they were meant to be there. Take the time to view the garden from all directions to ensure these items are suitably placed but, more importantly, be aware of the plants installed around them and their potential for growth to make sure these furnishings are not overwhelmed by the plant life in the future.

entertainment

2

FOR MOST OF US, ENTERTAINING is one of the key functions of our gardens, somewhere to interact with friends and family and an environment suited to relaxation and tranquillity. There are also sports to be enjoyed, whether a ball game on the lawn or tennis on your private court. All these features are about removing yourself from the confines of buildings and into an outdoor space tailored to your lifestyle.

Entertaining is about having fun and a successful design enables you to enjoy the experience of being a host to others. Innovation in design and the correct layout and placement of features will create an environment for all to enjoy.

As the architecture of homes has developed over the past 10 to 15 years, it has enhanced the indoor–outdoor lifestyle with open-plan designs and the use of large bi-fold doors and windows that are all aimed to the exterior space. The views from within the home should be a key factor when designing the outdoor areas. They should provide tranquillity but also entice movement towards them, from the front door, throughout the living areas and especially from the kitchen. More than ever the kitchen of today is the heart of the home, where people naturally gather at all times of day, and more than ever it has a strong connection with the garden outside.

Outdoor dining areas are one of the more frequent requests I receive from clients. With our love for the outdoors, it seems almost compulsory to cook and dine outside. Whether breakfast, lunch or dinner, enjoying a meal in the open air is a way of life. Modern landscape design has upgraded this function of the garden with inclusions to assist in a more enjoyable experience and increase the level of comfort. An outdoor lounge area with an open fire is an ideal location to retreat to after a meal, or to enjoy a drink or a quick nap, and heating also prolongs the use of the area throughout the seasons. Even the TV has made it outside and you can catch the news while cooking for the family or watch your favourite sporting event with friends without having to miss a moment.

The outdoors is where we all spent time when we were younger, exploring every corner of the yard and playing our make-believe games with friends. For those with children, the design of an outdoor space is the perfect opportunity to consider them within it and encourage them to enjoy the adventure and fantasy that a garden can bring to kids of all ages. There are many options available today when designing play areas that will ensure their fun and safety. Including an area for children as part of your garden not only provides them with a space for them to call their own, it gives you more time to enjoy yours.

ATMOSPHERE

A SUCCESSFUL OUTDOOR ENTERTAINING AREA is more than just correct layout and selection of elements and inclusions. You could have the most fantastic pool and dining area, with all the latest products installed, and it still could be missing the one thing that can't be bought from the store—atmosphere.

So how do you create atmosphere?

Atmosphere needs to be considered in any design and it is achieved when all of the elements are working as one to support and embrace the intended theme and use of the space. This is evident when you enter a beachside resort where the combination of all elements—pools, water features, view, etc—reinforce the beach culture and relaxing environment that the resort is promoting itself to be. The consistency of the furnishings and planting builds on the theme—even the style, colour and placement of the poolside chairs play a role in creating and maintaining the desired atmosphere.

The atmosphere of successfully designed entertaining areas makes you feel welcome. It invites you to do as you please and enables you to feel comfortable in an environment without challenges. The style and placement of elements within the space provide a sense of harmony, while the sound and movement of water add to the experience. You should feel the freedom to move to and from the designed areas without confusion, or even thought. The required pool equipment, sheds or storage areas will be out of sight, so that only the vision of the intended theme holds your attention.

When designing an entertaining area for resort-style living, I want the design to immediately communicate a lifestyle. This is achieved firstly with a layout that reflects the resort style, with functional and feature elements in a supporting role. The selection of all desired inclusions must be carefully considered—their shapes, sizes, colours and scale—and when correctly positioned they form the framework of the space. The integration of these elements is most important to a design's success and it is the real skill behind the art of landscaping. Many gardens have pools, water features, seating and paved areas but it is how these items connect and flow that enable them to be enjoyed at their best. As a design develops, the inclusion of furnishings and plant material that enhance a certain theme will bring an unspoken air of comfort to the space.

The atmosphere of resort-style living is created by all the chosen elements working together to convey the theme. The smooth blue tones of the water in the pool and the foliage colours of the leaves that surround it, the texture and colour of paving and walls, and even the fabric of cushions, all combine to reinforce the message. The furniture plays a critical role, too, as its selection and placement should clearly communicate its purpose. The result should be welcoming to those who enter the space.

If atmosphere is achieved during the daylight hours, it will only be enhanced when the sun goes down.

The introduction of outdoor lighting at night creates an evocative mood that only lighting can achieve, and also provides opportunities to highlight feature items in an exciting way. Foliage colours and textures will become more noticeable, and the movement of water even more pronounced as it catches and reflects the light. The contrasts from light to dark can be used to draw attention to certain areas, or deflect it. Lighting can be used to emphasize shapes, such as with furnishings like statues, but can also have a softening effect on hard materials. In numerous ways, lighting can play an important role in creating atmosphere and assisting to bring a design to its intended use.

The design of lights within the garden is an important consideration; however, I am personally more interested in the source of the light and the effect that it will achieve rather than the light fitting itself. I prefer lighting to be blended into the garden, reducing the visibility of the fittings unless they are required, such as for wall mountings or step treads and overhanging structures. Uplighting feature plants and elevated structures creates a smooth effect as the light blends out of view into the night sky after it has illuminated its desired feature. For special functions or events, the use of fire lamps will further enhance the atmosphere created and evoke visions of an island resort with lamps stretched along the beach. For a more intimate feel, the use of candles will provide the intended mood and the reflections of the small flames can be used to highlight water or nearby foliage.

Sound is also an integral element of atmosphere, whether it's the soothing notes of a trickling water feature or your favourite CD by the pool. The introduction of music to the space plays a role in creating atmosphere—it will support the style of the setting and also reflect its function. There are a growing number of weatherproof speakers which can be installed within the garden which will allow greater flexibility to incorporate music into outdoor spaces.

INDOOR-OUTDOOR

THE INTERACTION OF THE INDOORS and outdoors in modern home design is not just a trend, it is a realisation that additional rooms exist outside and that with the correct design and placement of selected items, the indoor and outdoor spaces can give strength to each other. A lifestyle is created with indoor–outdoor design, where the landscape of your property is not only the view from your home, it is an extension of your living environment.

The open-plan design of modern houses embraces the indoor–outdoor living concept. It enables a clearer vision of spaces available within the home, with fewer internal walls and more large windows and external doors, but also of the garden beyond it. In these designs, the garden is drawn into the home. Because of the clear vision of an open-plan, you have the impression of being in the garden while you are indoors. You can have the same relationship with nature, and experience the same feelings of the garden, surrounded by foliage and views, gentle breezes and the fragrance of flowers. In these designs, the sound of running water in the garden can be heard and seen when indoors, and the layout can even provide opportunities to incorporate the garden's water feature into the home design.

I enjoy opportunities to work with clients to enhance this relationship between indoors and outdoors, and to assist in taking the blend beyond its usual boundaries. Importantly, however, the garden design should create an environment that supports the room inside and extends that room's function to the outdoor space. Each living space within the home should have a strong relationship with the space outside it. Areas for living and eating and the kitchen should flow outdoors, both in function and style, with the design of the garden providing additional space to enjoy their activities. The view of the outdoor space from within and the blending of the areas also assists in making the rooms feel larger.

All rooms within the home will require a different treatment pending the home design and layout, but the same principles in translating the mood and function of that room to its outside space will apply. This is evident when designing courtyard spaces which flow from a bedroom: the mood and function of that room is of rest and relaxation so the garden design should be supportive of that purpose, not in conflict with it. The garden may include items of relaxation, such as seating or a day bed, placed in view, and the gentle flow of water could also be considered to provide a calming effect through sight and sound. The planting would also be less formal and structured, and would adopt a tranquil feel with soothing shapes, colours and textures, and soft foliage that rustles in the breeze. The floor product may also differ from what is used in other outdoor areas, with the introduction of timber or loose pebbles to add to the desired effect.

53

DINING

THE OUTDOOR DINING AREA HAS become one of a property's most valuable assets, no matter what its style, size or location, and its importance justifies careful consideration to its design. When created successfully, the location for outdoor dining will work effortlessly, drawing attention to itself and its function, making your dining experience a complete pleasure rather than a challenge. A well-designed dining area with comfortable furniture and a welcoming atmosphere will draw you into it more frequently and become a multi-purpose space—somewhere to enjoy a morning coffee, a talk on the phone or for children's homework.

The layout of the space is most influential on the design of the outdoor dining area. One the most common mistakes is not allowing enough room for the area to fulfil its intended use. When this happens, movement around the table becomes difficult, chairs need to be moved to allow access, and nearby plantings and water features become obstacles rather than elements that enhance the mood. The scale of the area should be established in the design phase and, especially in smaller spaces, all the elements within the dining area—the table, chairs, cooking unit, furnishings and features—will need to match that scale.

One of the best environments for outdoor dining is created when the area is housed within a custom-built gazebo or cabana structure and fitted with all the items required to enhance the ease and enjoyment of the experience. As a general rule, these structures are designed and constructed to reflect the home's architecture, but a themed structure of a more relaxed style can be considered if it is supported within the overall design. These areas should be designed with the neighbours in mind, providing walls or screening for privacy and to assist in the reduction of noise for those functions that run into the night.

The elements installed and the materials used within outdoor dining areas will be governed by the overall design themes, but should also serve the function of the space. For example, paving or timber decking for floors will make cleaning up easy after the dining is complete. With the kitchen nearby, and the inclusion of the fridge within the dining area, the ease and comfort of servicing your guests with drinks has moved up a level from the humble esky in the corner filled with ice. For those who enjoy entertaining frequently, an outdoor bar can be included in the design, perfect for enjoying drinks before moving onto dinner.

The importance of the placement of the dining table within the design should never be overlooked, and requires detailed investigation during the design phase. I have often seen the outdoor dining table placed right outside the back door of the home, which blocks the traffic flow in and out of the doorway and also hampers the view of the garden from within the home. This may be unavoidable in some designs and in smaller locations the choices for table placement may be limited; if so the bulk and scale of the furniture should be reduced to have less impact on its position.

The view from the dining table is also an important consideration, and should add to the experience. As with a good restaurant there are the good locations to sit with the best views and aspects and there are the bad locations that seem uncomfortable and lack atmosphere. The position of the dining table should relate to the design of the space, providing a clear vision of all its features as well as the opportunity to take in the detail when spending time there. If the property has a pool, it is important to have a clear vision of it from the dining location to ensure young children can be supervised as they will generally be in the pool longer than the adults.

The selection of your dining furniture will depend on the scale and style of the garden, but it is also an opportunity to express your intentions for the space. The outdoor dining experience is about relaxation and enjoying the company of others, so it is worthwhile taking the time to review a comfortable selection of furniture. The correct table and chair height, combined with soft furnishings such as additional cushions, will help to make the time spent there as enjoyable as possible. The outdoor dining experience also brings new opportunities to dress the table setting in creative ways. The ever-increasing selection of plates, cups and other related items that are designed for outdoor living ensures that you can put the finishing touches on any dining event.

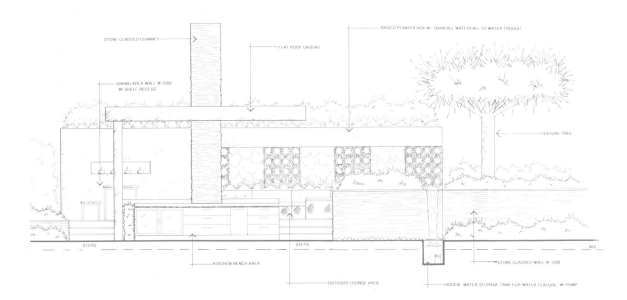

COOKING

THE PLEASURE OF OUTDOOR COOKING is enjoyed by most, and over the years this experience has been assisted by the design of more tailored environments complete with appliances that were once reserved for indoor kitchens. I consider the development of the outdoor kitchen to be a key factor in the evolution of resort-style living. These kitchens are designed not only as locations to cook the meal, but can also include all the necessary items and features to ensure that cooking for friends and family is convenient and enjoyable.

The location of an outdoor kitchen is central to a garden's design as its placement is affected by so many factors. With the weather to contend with, an outdoor kitchen is best installed with some form of covering to prolong its life span and to protect the appliances and features. For this reason it is often located close to the home or within a sheltered gazebo structure. The installation of lighting will allow the area to be used at night, and highlight it as a feature of the property. The layout and placement of all elements needs to be planned to ensure that everything serves its purpose and fits the scale of the space—so that you can move around, prepare, cook and serve a meal with minimal fuss and organisation.

All the equipment and conveniences of a kitchen that you enjoy within the home can also be enjoyed in the outdoors. There are many options for cooking units, from portable or built-in barbecues to custom-fitted stoves and ovens. The installation of a fridge means that food and drink can be stored onsite, and a sink with hot and cold water allows for convenient food preparation as well as cleaning. A dishwasher or microwave can be added for even greater convenience, especially on larger properties where the outdoor kitchen is some distance from the home. The inclusion of drawers and cupboards provides storage for cooking equipment, plates, cutlery and glasses, as well as any additional items that need storing or protection from the weather, while bench space is never under-used.

Including a purpose-built space for cooking provides even greater opportunities to experience the pleasures of outdoor living, regardless of whether the outdoor kitchen is of a grand culinary scale or conveniently compact. Not only does it prolong the time spent outdoors and reduce the need to move to and from the home while entertaining, it also supports the garden's general theme of relaxation and enjoyment.

PLAY

SOMEWHERE TO PLAY IS ONE of the garden's most important functions. We can all remember the time we spent outside as children, when the garden provided a place for games, riding bikes and running around, and a chance to get dirty. It was a place to interact with friends, discover the environment and simply imagine. To a child, the garden is a very important place so it is critical to consider their needs when you are designing the landscape around your home.

Through a careful approach, it is possible to customise play areas in the garden that children can take ownership of; these also add interest to a landscape and are pleasing to the eye. Lawn does not always have to be flat, it can have interesting contours that are fun. The inclusion of a cubby house or swing set is an opportunity to design a visual feature with selected plantings, while a trampoline may be installed so that it is level with the lawn, providing added safety and reducing its visibility. A sand pit attracts a great deal of use when children are younger, but usually becomes redundant when they grow up. This simple element of play can easily be incorporated into most garden designs, then re-developed into another feature or lawn when no longer needed.

Children will hurt themselves and that is part of growing up but the design of play areas, material selection and installation will play the most important role in their safety. Choose child-friendly materials wherever possible, such as soft rubber pavers or thick mulch material for the floor coverings. Spend the time to smooth the edges of timber used in construction to give a more rounded finish.

Special consideration must be given to pools and water features, as the risk they pose is one of the highest concerns for most parents. However, you can ensure the safety of children without compromising the visual quality of the design. Fencing should be considered as part of the pool design and incorporated with planting or other structures to lessen its impact and ensure it is a feature for the right reasons. There are many decorative options available, as well as freestanding walls that feature colour or texture and glass fencing which is especially suitable where a view is concerned.

The resort-style garden is also a great location for the big kids to play in. Paved areas and lawns around the pool and entertaining areas can host all sorts of sports and activities. The inclusion of a tennis court is not only functional for that game, but it can also serve as a multi-purpose area for other games to be played, whether football or basketball. A putting green can be incorporated in an area of lawn, and on large acreage properties the green could be extended into a private golf course with bunkers and fairways right outside your home.

3

relaxation

WE ALL RELAX IN OUR OWN individual ways. The notion of relaxation is different for everyone, and it also changes throughout each person's lifetime and with their surroundings. For some, relaxing may mean finding the quietest place in the garden, for others it could mean entertaining friends, or being in the pool with the kids climbing all over you. Maybe relaxation means all of those things to you, or something else altogether. What is important is that your garden is designed to cater to the way you choose to relax, with all the inclusions to assist in that outcome.

I have always loved the ability to just open the back door and take a wander in the backyard, to check on the latest growth in the plants and to enjoy the surroundings that have been created to capture my attention in line with my preferences. The opportunity to dive in the pool, pull up a chair or lie on the lawn is evident in the design of the space, reflecting some of my desired forms of relaxation. It also caters for the fact that my two small boys will soon appear beside me with a ball in hand or a game to take part in. All of these needs are taken into consideration in the design of the backyard, creating an environment that encourages me, my family and friends to relax.

Relaxation is an intrinsic part of resort-style living. It is a function of every inclusion in the outdoor space—the pool and spa, the outdoor dining and cooking areas, the plants, the furnishings— as well as the design and layout of the area itself. This style of living highlights the concept of a location to relax and unwind, with features tailored to the environment and to individual use.

Just as you would for your home, you need to think carefully about how to furnish your garden to create the most relaxing environment. Whether it's a simple bench tucked away under a shady tree or a full lounge setting complete with coffee table, sound system and lighting, the outdoor furniture you choose and the way you arrange it will impact on your ability to use the space.

As the seasons change so will the way you use the garden. However, the design of the space and its inclusions can ensure that you enjoy the garden's relaxing qualities all year round. Just as shade from trees keeps you cool in summer, an outdoor fireplace is an invaluable inclusion that prolongs the use of your garden in the colder months. A defining feature of resort-style living, a fireplace creates an atmosphere that embraces relaxation and comfort as you sit and watch the fire's entrancing flames.

INTIMACY

THE GARDEN IS A VERY INTIMATE location which provides a sense of security and privacy that is not often found indoors. In life we tend to travel from one building structure to another, whether from home to office, shops to schools, or airport to hotel. We spend a lot of time within buildings, limited by walls and a ceiling and surrounded by a lot of people who we do not know. For this reason our gardens have become invaluable locations where we can retreat and reflect on those things that are most important to us all. We can choose what it looks like, how it functions and who is invited into it, giving us a sense of control of the space and of our lives. A garden does this by providing an instant impression of intimacy, welcoming you into a space that is created just for you and far removed from the pace of daily life.

Intimacy is about creating a mood. An intimate environment allows you to sink into the relaxing atmosphere that has been created and take time out for yourself whenever you choose. Here, the walls of buildings are replaced by plant life in a variety of shapes and colours to tease the eye, while their tactile qualities and fragrance will also stir the senses. Gentle breezes that move the plant material back and forth give life to the space, and also add natural sounds that are only achieved by the foliage and branches of plants brushing against each other, creating an atmosphere that is rarely experienced indoors. With the ceiling removed and replaced by open sky over the garden, you can experience the warmth of the sun, which is naturally comforting, and enjoy the shapes created by the clouds.

The intimate mood of a garden embraces relaxation with the creation of a tranquil atmosphere through its overall design, and the features and furnishings of the space should also be tailored to achieve this. Screening and plants can be used to block any undesirable views, while the inclusion of a gentle flowing water feature not only assists in the tranquil mood but can also mask unwanted noises from the home or nearby roads. Selected sculpture pieces can be used as focal points and to gently furnish the area. In the evening, the atmosphere can be enhanced with the installation of lighting, illuminating and highlighting tree trunks and feature items and creating amazing displays of colours and textures not normally seen during the day. As the seasons change so does the mood of your garden and this can bring new opportunities to tailor the environment towards relaxation. On cold winter evenings, the inclusion of a fireplace in your outdoor lounge room will ensure your comfort and provide a cosy atmosphere for a night under the stars with someone special.

RETREAT

YOUR GARDEN IS LIKE NO OTHER place. It is your personal retreat. It's a space where you can truly be yourself, where you can smell the fresh air, interact with family and friends, and feel alive. It is a safe location where children can play and discover plant, animal, bird and insect life, and where their imaginations can create worlds of make-believe. It is a place where we can sit still, a place to wander, a place to stop and talk to each other. It is an environment where you can do as you please, without having to conform to the socially acceptable rules that we abide by in our daily lives, where you can escape when you need to, to reflect on the things that are most important.

The garden provides us with the opportunity to remove ourselves from the normal schedule of our daily lives, to relax and unwind away from the usual distractions of busy lives and lack of time. The imported noises of the home and world outside fade into the background and the sounds of moving water and the rustle of plants and foliage take its place. Sunlight warms us in the cooler seasons, while overhanging trees and plants provide shade and shelter in the summer. Infinite tones of green surround us, with contrasting colours and textures, adding to the relaxing environment and the sense of escape that a garden brings.

The creation of a retreat in the garden is a valuable addition that greatly enhances the relaxation potential and overall design. This element of resort-style living can be included in any garden, large or small. Whether the seclusion of a courtyard space with a single bench seat, a purpose-built area that serves as an outdoor lounge room, or a secret garden hidden away in the corner of a larger property, it is the design and furnishing of the space that will clearly communicate its message.

The layout and aspect of the retreat area are important considerations. To ensure a tranquil and private environment that embraces relaxation, you may need to install shelter and screening with plants or other structures such as freestanding walls, especially if the design includes outdoor bathing areas. The overhanging foliage of trees create an environment of seclusion, and also the opportunity to introduce shade-loving plants that can provide a new experience with the colours and textures available. Elements within the space should also appeal to your relaxation needs. The furnishings should be functional and uncomplicated, but they should also look and feel inviting. The inclusion of a water feature or sculpture can also bring a personal connection to the space.

A secret garden can enhance the notion of a retreat, separating you even further from everyday life and transporting you into an environment of pure seclusion. Due to its separate location from other areas on a property, it can also be an opportunity for a different style and selection of furnishings and plant material.

An important feature of the secret garden is the experience of discovery. It is the journey through the garden that prepares you for the seclusion within. The path to the secret garden could take you over a rolling lawn to a distant location, or wind through a grove of closely planted trees, or simply lead you away from the main thoroughfare into a hidden location nearby where the structured and tailored materials start to be become replaced with informal paths and plantings that suggest a mood of relaxation.

A secret garden should always be inviting to enter. It should have a presence of tranquillity. The furniture in these gardens is often of a minimal style, such as a simple park bench or chairs, so that they don't detract from the pure purpose of the space. The placement of seating should entice you to sit and take in your surroundings. A water feature can act as a focal point, as well as provide soothing sounds. Alternatively, the location may be ideal for displaying a selection of sculptures. In a garden that is separated from the main areas of the property, you can experience a greater relationship with the plants within it, as they will not be competing with others found closer to the home. Fragrant plants are especially highlighted, and provide the space with a distinct mood that you will associate with relaxing.

LOUNGE

WE ALL LOVE OUR LOUNGE in the home. This is where we often end up at the end of the day, where we sit back and relax which soon develops into lying down and having a nap. The lounge room is where we are drawn to when friends arrive for a coffee, or for drinks after dinner, because of the level of comfort and atmosphere of relaxation it provides. But this level of comfort is not exclusive to the indoors, and in fact it can be created equally, if not enhanced, when taken outside.

An outdoor lounge area has the same function as one inside the house, but the relaxation takes place in an environment that is unique and interacts with the features of the landscape. It embraces the concept of resort-style living, providing a fully functional outdoor space tailored to your needs. As soon as you step into the space, the visual impact of the design reinforces luxury and relaxed living, and the purpose of the area is immediately apparent. Views from the area are tranquil, and the layout is intimate but also allows easy movement to and from the space. The selection of furnishings and other inclusions reinforces the relaxed message, providing somewhere to eat, drink and play comfortably.

The role of the lounge setting in influencing the feel of the space is of immense importance, and the design and scale of the space will decide the style of the seating furniture. There are many outdoor lounge suites available for purchase that will be in keeping with the look and feel of your garden's design, and some have the additional benefit of being modular, which means they can be rearranged according to particular functions. Lounge settings can also be built into the garden's design, ensuring that they are completely tailored to the size and style of the garden as well as its purpose. Custom-built seating can be constructed from various materials, such as masonry or timber, to complement other materials used in the garden, and with the addition of soft furnishings they can be dressed up or down to suit any occasion.

The layout of the lounge furniture also requires detailed consideration in an outdoor space. Furniture pieces should be placed to encourage leisure and comfort, but also interaction, just as they are in an indoor lounge room. With the general lack of television outside, lounge settings can face each other, enabling closer interaction. For more contemporary designs I have constructed U-shaped lounge suites. This layout provides the opportunity for a larger group of people to interact with each other but with enough space to stretch out and enjoy the atmosphere. In courtyards and smaller gardens that are limited in space, the scale of the furnishings can be reduced, for example using a set of single chairs instead of lounges, without compromising the atmosphere of relaxation. Of course a low table to put your coffee, snack or feet on will complete the scene.

The introduction of other selected furnishings and plantings will not only increase the level of contentment in the outdoor lounge area, but also support the desired theme. For example, in a Bali-style garden, a day bed made of hand-carved timber will play a role in defining the theme, as well as creating a highly sought-after location for lazing around with the Sunday paper, while the addition of textured foliage in a tropical-style planting will reinforce the look and feel of the retreat.

I often include water features in outdoor lounge areas to enhance the tranquil environment. Like all elements in these designs, water features need to support the purpose and theme of the location, therefore fast-flowing water features are best avoided as the sound of the water can be loud and make conversations difficult, and they also bring an undesirable energy to the location. The gentle sound of water surrounding and embracing the lounge area is much more conducive to relaxation, such as the soothing backdrop that is created as water trickles down a wall of glass mosaic tiles.

The planting of these areas greatly influences the atmosphere. Plants should be selected to create the impression of your own private oasis, adding to the feeling of seclusion and retreat. They should also define the outdoor lounge by providing natural fragrance, colours and textures that are not normally found within the home. The balance of planting and comfortable furnishings, with the warmth of the sun or the light of the moon at night, communicates the desired use of the space and transforms it into a relaxing retreat that is the essence of outdoor living.

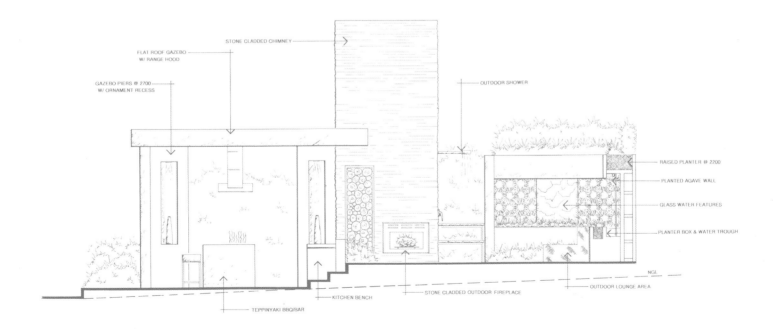

HEATING

MY LOVE FOR THE USE OF fire in the garden is no secret and anyone who has experienced the atmosphere of an outdoor fireplace will be equally enthusiastic. The outdoor fireplace is an amazing feature in the garden, and plays a key role in the expression of a resort-style living design. It has a practical purpose, extending the use of the garden at night particularly as the seasons change to the colder months, and provides a mood that only fire can bring. An outdoor fireplace also has an almost primal function in its ability to attract people towards it, a quality which can be developed wisely in the design of the garden, using it as a directional tool and focal point within the overall landscape.

The outdoor lounge area has a natural relationship with the fireplace, allowing you to enjoy the warmth and atmosphere the fire provides while you relax in comfort. There are so many ways in which fire can be incorporated into the garden, from a simple bowl that is brought out when required and stored away when not in use, with the added option of moving it to suit the occasion, to a custom-built fireplace that is a central feature of the garden's entertaining area. A fire pit set into the ground and surrounded by built-in seating in a circular design, which allows people to sit facing each other just as they do around a camp fire, is particularly suitable for resort-style designs. A fire pit can be constructed beside your outdoor entertaining area, or it could be a separate retreat that is hidden down a path or behind another garden structure, giving the feature a sense of adventure as you discover and experience it.

As much as I enjoy all styles of fire use in the garden, I do have a preference for the bold statement that a chimney structure can bring to a landscape. Where the design of a property allows it, an open fireplace and chimney can be integrated into an outdoor living space that also houses the kitchen and dining areas, such as in a gazebo. The design of the chimney provides the opportunity to introduce a stone feature into the landscape, as a focal point that draws attention and also as a location to mount the showerhead or other items requiring height. Incorporating a space for cut logs in the fireplace's design enhances the theme created while also being a practical storage location for the timber. With some designs measuring 4–5 metres in height, the chimney of a fireplace is also a perfect opportunity to add scale and structure to a garden, capturing your attention and defining the environment created.

BATHING

WITH THE PRIVACY THAT CAN be created in a garden space, I encourage the installation of an outdoor bathing area whenever possible. Some clients have questioned the need for a shower or bathtub in the garden, but they soon discover the unique feeling of relaxation that outdoor bathing can bring. Just as you would find in a luxurious hotel resort or health spa, the outdoor shower or bath provides a location to enjoy the movement of water on your body, surrounded by the plants and gentle breezes of the garden. This can be experienced in the day or night, in all seasons, providing a personal retreat within easy reach of your home.

In recent years, the outdoor bathroom has been embraced in many styles of landscape design, but it has always had a defining role in the resort-style living environment where design is tailored to function and has a relationship with the use of the area. The inclusion of an outdoor bathing area, whether with a shower or bathtub or both, brings additional value to the use of the garden and provides a personal and intimate connection with it. It builds on the overall design theme, reinforcing the garden as an extension of the home and a place for items that have long been considered as suitable only for indoors.

An outdoor shower can be incorporated into most garden designs as it requires less space than a bathtub or spa. The shower has a practical function—providing a tailored location for rinsing off after being in the pool or spa, or for cleaning up after working in the garden, preventing the need to tip-toe through the house on your way to the bathroom, or simply for refreshing yourself after work or play—but it also adds to the garden's atmosphere of outdoor living.

The outdoor bathtub differs from a shower, and even from a spa, as it is generally more of a personal item. It is a location to sit and soak, allowing time to pass without care. The stillness of the water allows you to take in the natural sounds and the movement of foliage, while lighting or candles cast unique shapes and shadows. In a bathtub, you can take the time to enjoy the sensation of cool air on your skin, and you can lean back and gaze at the stars in the open sky above.

Privacy is an important issue with outdoor bathrooms, as the experience will only be enjoyed if you feel relaxed about baring all in your backyard. We are so used to the privacy of an indoor bathroom, with doors and windows that can be closed, and the outdoor bathing area has the same needs. With the right design considerations and screening from plants and structures, however, you can create a location where you can enjoy the experience of getting back to nature without challenging your comfort zone.

97

water

4

THE PRESENCE OF WATER WITHIN any garden adds life, movement, sound and tranquillity to the created environment, but in resort-style living water is a central element of a property and often determines its design. Water features can take so many forms, from a simple birdbath providing a drink and cool spot for wildlife to pools and spas or expansive water courses. It can be the focal point of a garden area, or designed to surround you completely once within a particular space. The size and style of a water feature will be determined by the scale and theme of the area, but whether large or small, it brings an opportunity to add a personal touch to the garden as well as communicate the intentions of the design.

Pools are one of the most common ways of including water in the outdoor space, and it has been a true passion of mine over the years to design contemporary pools that are beyond a place to cool down. A well-designed pool area can provide a great learning environment for children where they feel comfortable to develop their swimming skills, while providing parents with seating and a place to supervise and interact. Spas are also features that bring great opportunities in design; they also extend your time in the garden through the changing seasons and are a great place to relax with friends.

Water is generally one of the easiest elements to integrate into a garden, regardless of size or setting, but any water feature, whether a pond, pool, spa or simple bowl, has to be carefully considered to ensure it is sustainable for the long term. Even though there are many products on the market to assist in keeping the water clean and flowing, most, if not all, water features will require some level of maintenance. Evaporation in any water feature is commonly overlooked, but can be easily solved with additions such as top-up valves or with designs that access rainwater. Including your water feature in your garden's maintenance schedule will ensure it operates at the same level as when it was installed and also provides the sensory impact it was designed for.

While water features do play a vital role as a visual element in a garden's design, they can be practical as well. In some cases, the water feature can be the life source for birds and wildlife, as well as for plant material, and contribute to the health and sustainability of the garden. On some of the larger acreage properties I have worked on, I have had the opportunity to deal with the important factor of water collection and its re-use. As water becomes more precious than ever, it is even more critical for the landscape to be designed with the catchment, storage and redistribution of water as an essential function. This involves drainage design and contour grading, to ensure the maximum catchment to storage tanks, or the development of dams and artificial creek systems. These designs not only provide a water storage facility and the mechanisms to move large volumes of water, they also create an environment for nature to call home.

POOLS

A SWIMMING POOL brings endless opportunities to the design potential of any property. The pool's design can be a strong indication of the desired theme or style of the garden and opens the door to the movement of water within it. The shape and size of the pool is governed by the area of your property, but sometimes what can seem like a challenging site can bring new and exciting options. A pool can be located in a purpose-built area of your property, or it can be designed to be an integral part of the home, built against the building, and it can even make its way into the home.

In a design that embraces resort-style living, the pool is more than just a place to swim. It forms the centre piece, and the design of the space works around it. Any pool can be incorporated into a resort-style theme, as it is not the shape or size of the pool that has an impact on the design—it is the effect that a large body of blue water creates, and how this is used, that makes it such a strong focal point. The inclusion of a spa, swim-up wet bar or flowing waterfalls will add to the overall impression. Importantly, how the pool is surrounded by plants, hard materials, lighting and furnishings will play a stronger role in communicating the resort-style theme.

Pool shapes have been influenced by trends over the years and recently the straight-line pool has become more common. Often now if curves are introduced they are of a controlled nature based on a radius. The shape of the pool should be based on its surroundings and how it will best suit the property. Every pool has its challenges to deal with but the time spent in the design phase will ensure its success during construction.

A pool is only as good as what surrounds it so it should be designed as part of the landscape, complementing the scale of the space, which will ensure its true integration. This is most evident when installing the pool fence. If the fencing is considered during the design phase, it can be selected to provide the required safety without interfering with the overall vision of the pool from the home and within the garden. There are many available materials for pool fencing, such as glass, that will be in the pool's style but will not detract from the landscape. Pending your local council's regulations, the pool body itself or freestanding walls can form part of the pool fence, creating a 'vanishing edge' design. Importantly, the location of the pool filter and other equipment shouldn't be forgotten in the design process, to ensure that it doesn't interfere with the view or the use of the area.

When designing a pool as part of a resort-style garden, you have a unique opportunity to review the inclusions that would suit your family and the way you would like to relax and entertain. Swim-up ledges within the pool serve a number of purposes, providing a place to rest when in the water, while also being a great feature for kids to learn to swim. These ledges have been increasing in size over the years, as more people discover the enjoyment of having a shallow area in the pool to lie around and talk with friends and family.

Water features as part of the pool design aren't necessary to achieve a resort style, but they can bring an additional element of life to the body of water. The design of the pool will play a major role in the selection of water features, but the movement of water within the pool can be achieved in many ways—whether by a freestanding wall with water flowing down it, a bubbling fountain, or the introduction of levels with water running between them.

The installation of plants around the pool softens the effect of hard materials and strengthens the desired theme. Detailed descriptions of suitable plants for poolside settings are given in the section 'Plants' (page 129), and in Chapter 5 in 'Grow' (page 143), but in general the best choices will be determined by considering the pool's aspect and location. Because pool areas are usually sun-drenched and warm, the selected plants should revel in those conditions, as well as tolerate the occasional splash of chlorine or salt from the pool water. Deciduous plants and others that frequently drop foliage are recommended to be avoided, to reduce maintenance of the area and therefore increase your enjoyment of the pool. Potted plants around the pool can be used as focal points, but will need attention to watering. For a resort-style pool setting, there are many choices in plant selection, but the inclusion of foliage colour and structure always has a place.

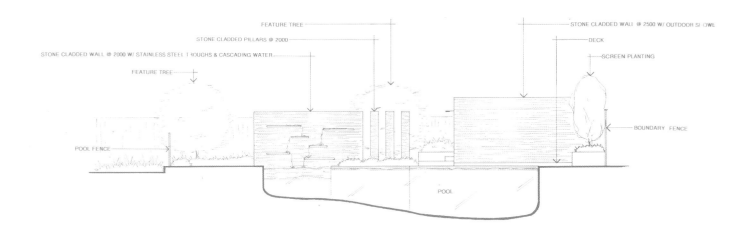

AN OUTDOOR SPA BRINGS a unique opportunity to create a location that removes you from the usual surrounds of the home and places you into an environment of pure enjoyment and relaxation. During the day as well as the evening, and in all seasons, a spa is an inviting destination to be shared with family and friends. The intimacy and relaxation potential of an outdoor spa makes it an ideal location for entertaining, enjoying conversation and drinks, and also as a romantic location for two. Time seems to pass without a care as you enjoy the warmth of the bubbling water, with the coolness of the air in the still of the evening.

The location of the spa and its surrounds will need to be considered carefully in the design phase of the garden, as it should provide an atmosphere of serenity and relaxation as well as convenience. For each property the best location for a spa will differ, depending greatly on how you would prefer to view the spa and interact with it. The spa may be the feature of the overall design, drawing your attention from inside the home, with a strong connection to the landscape. Or it could be positioned out of view, in a private oasis surrounded by lush planting. Wherever the preferred location, the view from the spa—whether natural or created—should aid in the relaxation experience, and a strong planting scheme surrounding it will provide a sense of sanctuary.

Other important features of the spa's location also need to be considered during the design phase to ensure that the area functions as a special space to retreat to within your garden. Sometimes the spa is attached to a pool, which provides opportunities for the movement of water between the two, and allows for the creative integration of their designs. Roof structures over the spa create a sense of enclosure, and apart from allowing the space to be used in all weather, they can also play a major role in increasing the privacy of the area if required. Lighting extends the time which can be spent in the spa, and can also highlight the design, as well as greatly enhance the night atmosphere in line with a particular occasion. Furnishings also add to the experience of relaxing or entertaining, from the simplicity of somewhere to put your clothes and towel, or bench seating which allows interaction between those who are in the spa and those who aren't, to the ultimate convenience of a nearby shower, or a fridge for topping up your drinks.

As with pools, the location of the operating equipment is just as important as the location of the spa itself, and needs to be considered in the development of the area's design. If the area is small you may consider hiding the equipment behind a freestanding wall: the wall could be used to display a feature item; or it could be a feature in itself, painted in a colour that adds contrast to the garden; or seating or a shower may be integrated. These features will draw your attention to the wall for the right reasons, and not because of what is located behind it.

WATER FEATURES

WATER MOVEMENT IN THE GARDEN brings life and energy to a space. It draws your attention to a location, and produces an atmosphere that is unique. The sound of moving water, as expressed in nature by a gentle flowing creek, will always beg investigation and gives comfort that life is around you.

I have always loved the design of gardens with water features. With the availability of so many interesting materials on the market today, there are no limits as to how you can incorporate water in your garden. Within a resort-style theme, the water feature can play a leading role in communicating the impression of the designed space, and provide a connection between the design and the landscape. The space available and the contours of each property will determine how this can best be achieved, as no two properties are the same, but there are opportunities for new ideas every time a water feature is requested and I believe that this is one of the most rewarding elements of landscape design.

Even though water features can create an outstanding visual impact in a garden's design, the interaction with water is what inspires me most. I enjoy designing water features to be part of a living space, and not just an item for ornamentation. I love the idea of walking over water, whether on a bridge or stepping stones or even a glass floor, as it enables a close connection with the water. The best example of this element of interaction was a design I created for an entertaining area where the water flowed between two sheets of glass that formed the dining table before falling into a pond below. This design allowed me to integrate the movement of water, and all the stunning visual elements it brings, into a practical and commonly used item.

The placement of a water feature has a close relationship to the garden's design, both as a visual feature and in helping to create direction. Suitable locations for water features will differ, but will always relate to the layout of the home and landscape, the function of the water feature and the intended style of the design. Even within each property there will be various locations, apart from the main outdoor living areas, which will require an individual approach. The front entry to a property, for example, is a popular location for a water feature to greet visitors, and it can provide a hint of what they will see once within the property. Water features also bring feelings of tranquillity and relaxation indoors if positioned where they can be viewed and heard from rooms in the house. Wherever the feature is placed, however, the sight and sound of the water should always draw you towards it.

The design and construction of a water feature that is customised to your property provides the opportunity to create a unique statement like no other. Over the years the range of commercially available and manufactured water features has increased, and while these do have some limitations in material use and colour selection, generally there will be many options in the market that will be in keeping with your garden's style. A customised water feature, however, is only limited by the space available and the preferred budget.

These individually tailored features can create a strong and dynamic statement, but also interact with the overall look, shape and feel of the design. Construction materials can be selected to complement the garden's design and theme, and to also enhance the uniqueness of the feature, such as when glass and stainless steel are integrated with stone. A customised water feature is ideal for difficult locations and small spaces where the manufactured versions may not be the correct scale or fit into the desired layout. It also provides great opportunities to feature water throughout the entire garden and even in the house, and bring all the elements of the design closer together by connecting the different bodies of water. For properties with a pool, this can be integrated with the water feature to allow the water to flow from feature to feature, leading the eye towards the main visual element of the pool.

While water features are invaluable elements of garden design, their maintenance should not be forgotten. Although they generally require very little maintenance compared to other areas of the garden, some basic care will ensure the feature continues to serve the purpose it was installed for. For water features that are constructed in a similar manner to a pool, with the use of steel and concrete along with pumping and cleaning systems, a plan should be devised to prevent damage to equipment and other parts of the feature. Check the pump every six months, to ensure it is free of debris which can overload its mechanisms. It is also recommended that any basins and water holding areas are drained and cleaned every year or two; this ensures the water is kept healthy, and makes the feature look as good as new. Basic maintenance doesn't take much time, but it will have a lasting effect on the reliability of your water feature and your enjoyment of it.

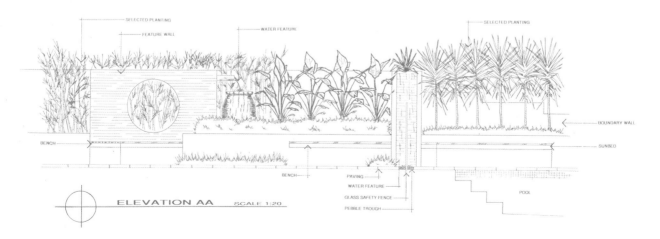

ELEVATION AA   SCALE 1:20

PONDS

PONDS AS WATER FEATURES PLAY an important role in the visual attraction of a garden design, but they also have a specific purpose and that is to re-create nature. For large or small properties a pond can provide a habitat for fish and plant life, as well as provide a water source for birdlife and animals, and over time a natural ecosystem forms, while its inclusion in a garden provides you with a location for tranquillity and relaxation.

Within a resort-style design, a pond is usually constructed as a retreat. The location of a pond will vary depending on the property's available spaces; it may be visible from the main entertaining area, but it can also be hidden with elements that will tease you to discover its location. The design of the pond and surrounding area is generally of an informal nature, with a relaxed planting theme that creates a peaceful atmosphere. A pond brings the opportunity to use natural products such as rocks and stones to line its floor and edges, as well as creating an environment for water plants and aquatic life, while shade from trees that overhang the pond will provide shelter and comfort to all who enter the environment, including wildlife.

Many of the ponds I have designed and built would not be called a pond by a lot of people: they often hold more than 1 million litres of water and are usually part of an artificial creek system that allows the water to be moved, turned and aerated. Generally, on these acreage estates, the main pond is located at the lowest part of the property, allowing a greater collection of water, and this also enables the installation of multiple ponds and creek beds to flow from a higher position down towards it. These watercourses form a stunning display and make a bold design statement, but they are also positioned to be the life source of the property, collecting every drop of rain available and transporting it to be stored for re-use in irrigation systems that ensure the survival of the property's plant life.

No matter what the pond size or location, however, the same principles of construction and design will apply. Lining the pond with a rubber membrane or similar material will assist in the quality of water while preventing leaks from occurring. Planting in and around the pond is soft and natural, with overhanging trees to create shade and shelter. To mimic nature as closely as possible, large rocks should be carefully positioned along the banks of the pond or creek, while smaller pebbles line the floors. Walls can be added on the sides of the pond, providing an opportunity to create a dramatic waterfall. Bridges and hardwood pontoons can also be introduced to allow greater interaction with the bodies of water, as well as access; and on larger properties, bridges can be combined with the driveway to wind through and around the creek and pond system. With the addition of lighting, the pond design is transformed at night, and any neighbouring distractions fade into the background: whether uplighting the pond's banks and the trees around it, highlighting structures, or simply reflecting off the water's surface.

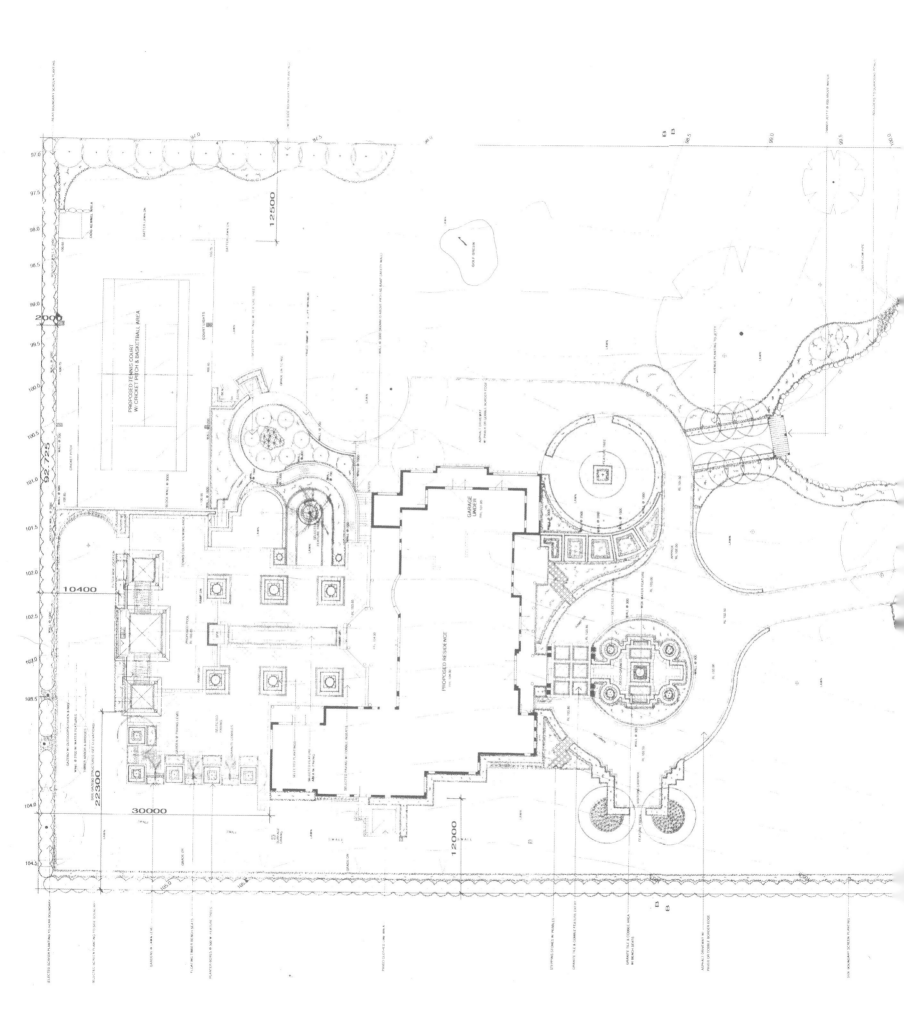

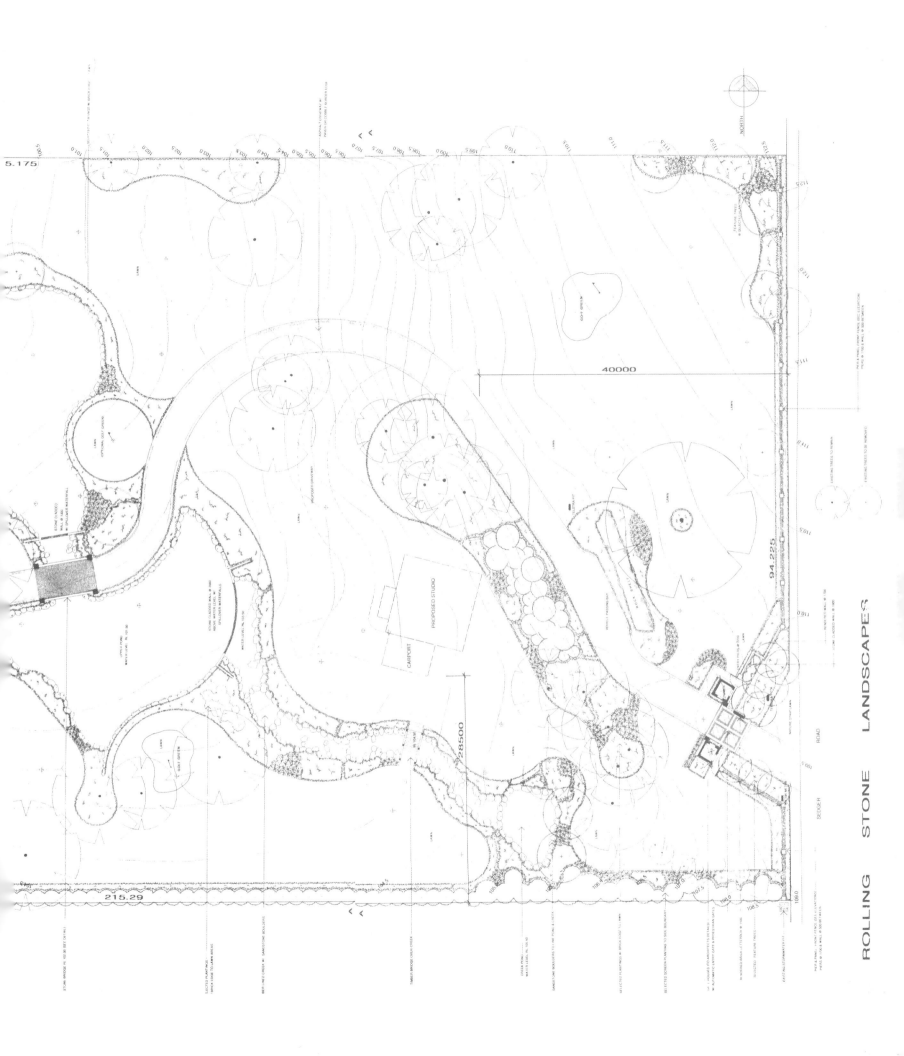

ROLLING STONE LANDSCAPES

PLANTS

WITH ANY WATER FEATURE, POND OR POOL, the selection and placement of plants is a key element in its completion and communication of an intended theme. In design, plants are the soft furnishings for the hard elements of a garden, and they have the added benefit of being a living element that grows, flowers and matures with the garden. Each body of water will have a different selection of plants that best suits its design and use, but in general plants should firstly be considered for their suitability to the proposed area and its aspect, ensuring their successful growth, as well as the way they relate to the elements within a design.

The selection of plants for pond settings will depend on the style of the pond, but the overall look is usually a soft and natural one. A blend in colour and texture will add interest to the planting, and the installation of trees with foliage that overhangs the pond provides shade and shelter. There should be movement in the planting when the breeze blows, and it should have some attraction to wildlife to reinforce the design's intentions of a re-created natural environment. The inclusion of grasses and water reeds will always be a natural choice for pond settings, bringing form and scale to the design while providing shelter for wildlife: taller and medium-growing species such as *Pennisetum* (Fountain Grass), *Cyperus* (Papyrus), *Dietes* (Wild Iris) or *Carex* (Sedge) can be planted in clumps around a large pond, or with a smaller pond they can be grouped in one corner; while the softer, lower-growing types like *Liriope* (Lily Turf) and *Acorus* (Sweet Flag) will always look in place as their foliage hangs gently over the pond edge.

The inclusion of planting in a water feature brings it to life, and aquatic plants are ideal for ponds and other bodies of fresh water. There are many options to choose from, depending on the climate of your garden, with a selection of foliage shapes, flowers and growth habits to suit your needs. *Nymphaea* (Waterlilies) are among the most popular of water-growing plants, with the tranquil look of their rounded floating leaves as well as their beautiful flowers in a range of colours.

For a poolside setting, *Strelitzia* (Bird of Paradise) is a great architectural plant with its upright habit, large leaves and striking orange flowers that stand in full view above the plant; it also has a long flowering period and is a very hardy plant around pools. *Cycas revoluta* (Japanese Sago Palm) makes a great statement if used as an accent plant, whether as a single focal point to draw attention to a design feature around the pool, or in pairs between steps or to define paved areas; this slow-growing plant requires very little maintenance. Another feature plant that is easy to grow is the well-loved frangipani (*Plumeria*), and its beautiful fragrant flowers perfectly complement the relaxing atmosphere of a pool. For plants to create a rich and lush landscape around the pool, the selection is very broad but do consider those with contrasting foliage colour such as *Tradescantia spathacea* (Boat Lily or Moses-in-the-cradle), a small plant with soft leaves that are dark green on one side and striking purple on the other; as well as the inspiring range of *Phormium* (New Zealand Flax), *Cordyline* and *Dracaena* that have outstanding foliage colour.

5

living

A RESORT-STYLE GARDEN IS A PLACE for outdoor living. It has been designed with function in mind, for entertaining friends and family, and with all the modern conveniences to satisfy your lifestyle needs, but it is also a space where you can truly be yourself, relax and enjoy the comfort of the sun and the plant life around you. In a resort-style design, the correct level of thought has been invested into every area of the garden, from the inclusions through to the soil and drainage requirements. The furnishings have been selected and their placement has been carefully considered for use. So now it's time to start living.

One of the best qualities of the resort-style garden is that all the items you require for entertaining or relaxing are in place, ready to fulfil their purpose with little to no preparation required. The outdoor kitchen is equipped with all the appliances and inclusions that you need to be a grand host, whether the occasion is large or small, and enjoy the time you spend doing it. The dining table is of a suitable size, with comfort considered in its selection, enabling a long and enjoyable dining experience with those closest to you. Lighting highlights all the elements that make up the view, while extending the time you spend in the created environment. At the push of a button, you can heat the spa to a perfect temperature so that once you have finished dining, the conversation can continue into the night in a unique venue tailored to your relaxation.

The fridge is nearby so your glass is always topped up, and there's a shower to refresh you after you get out of the spa. To see out the night, you can retreat to the outdoor lounge, where comfortable furnishings await you. If the temperature drops, the outdoor fireplace is ready to light, and this not only deals with the cold but also adds to the atmosphere already created. In your own garden, all of these luxuries of resort living are there for you at any time of day or night, whenever you need them.

Importantly, take a balanced approach between the time you spend caring for the garden and the time you spend living in it. Resort-style designs can require much less maintenance than some other garden styles, but caring for and maintaining your garden will add value to your property and reinforce the desired theme and lifestyle it was created for. You begin to know your garden as it matures, you see the results of your pruning efforts as new flushes of foliage burst through, you become aware of how your plants are flowering compared to previous years and take an interest in their success. I have found that even those who don't consider themselves gardeners soon develop an interest in the growth and health of their plants. Time spent maintaining the garden, shared with the family, can be a very relaxing and rewarding experience, and provides you with a stronger connection to the environment that you call home.

SENSES

THE GARDEN IS A LIVING ENVIRONMENT, influenced at every moment by the movements of the sun and wind and by the seasons. It excites all of our senses, providing us with experiences that make us feel alive, whether it's the sound of the wind rustling through leaves, the smell of a wood fire, or the feel of raindrops on your skin.

Of all the senses, sight is the first affected by the garden. The vision of the garden should instantly communicate the purpose of the space, as well as the story told by its theme. An inviting seat surrounded by lush planting sends a message of seclusion and retreat, the presence of a body of blue water is immediately cooling, while the sight of a fireplace evokes thoughts of intimacy and warmth. When placed in our line of sight, these features and inclusions provide a clear impression of what the garden is offering, and they also invite us to enter the scene.

The colours we see have an amazing impact on how we feel. In the garden, the colours of installed elements assist in creating the overall picture, but it is the colours of the planting that has the greatest impact on our senses. Even if flowers aren't a dominant part of the garden's design, the range of foliage plants available can be used to create stunning colour effects for almost any desired theme. Foliage plants can provide so many shades of green, as well as silver, cream, red, burgundy, blue and even black; and their variegated forms further extend the selection. Foliage also brings seasonal displays, and deciduous plants with colourful autumn leaves are a highlight of any garden, as well as the wintry colours of their bark which can be enjoyed once the leaves have fallen.

The effects of light also influence our sense of sight. Whether natural or created, light can determine the atmosphere of the garden, as well as our moods. The movement of the sun as it rises and sets will dramatically change the way the garden appears and feels. Morning sunlight is gentle, highlighting the tips of foliage and sparkling on water; while in the afternoon, strong contrasts between light and shadows start to appear, and the garden's plants and structures are boldly highlighted. Artificial lighting takes over at night to define the atmosphere and extend the time we spend outside. The inclusion of lighting provides opportunities to draw attention to features and areas of the garden, but also to create a sensory experience.

Like sight, our sense of smell has a strong connection with our emotions and memories. The unmistakable scent of freshly cut lawn, the smell of woodsmoke, or the perfume of a favourite flower can all provoke thoughts of particular times and places in our lives. Plants, of course, provide fragrances that enhance the garden's sensual qualities, and with the wide selection available they can even be installed to change as the seasons rotate. Importantly, scented plants should be positioned in the garden where you can frequently enjoy them, such as around entertaining areas and along pathways, but also near doorways and windows where their fragrance can naturally drift throughout the home. Plants with strongly scented flowers such as jasmine (*Jasimum*), mock orange (*Murraya*), gardenia (*Gardenia*) and frangipani (*Plumeria*) are especially suitable for resort-style gardens as they support the design theme and are easy to care for.

Gardens are full of both natural and created sounds and these work together to provide a fitting backdrop to the designed environment. The natural sounds are unique to each location, provided by birds and other wildlife, the wind as it moves the plants and their foliage, and the flowing of water. The collection of created sounds in the garden is produced by your enjoyment of it—water splashing in the pool, food cooking in the outdoor kitchen, wine bottles being opened, the crackle of the fireplace, and laughter, the most welcome sound of all, confirming that people are happy and the design has provided the location and facilities for this as intended.

Due to the importance of water to our survival, we have a strong bond with it and the sound of its movement provides comfort to us all. However, moving water makes different tones and so the volume of water movement requires consideration to ensure it is in keeping with the desired feeling of the garden. A gentle trickle of water will provide a tranquil atmosphere, while a fast-moving waterfall has an energetic and more powerful effect, creating a sound that takes a leading role in the environment. Depending on how it flows, the sound of water will evoke different moods and responses.

The sensory experience of taste can be well catered for in a resort-style garden. The addition of a vegetable garden or edible plants is welcome in many landscapes, but it perfectly complements the concept of an outdoor kitchen and supports the function of the designed space which is a key factor of the resort style. Food-producing plants can also be included in the overall design, adding convenience and a personal touch to the lifestyle theme. Whether the flavour of a freshly picked passionfruit added to ice cream or a lemon squeezed over your seafood, the taste of food grown at home is incomparable and strengthens the bond between you and your environment.

For many people, the sense of touch is what they most enjoy about being outdoors, whether it's the softness of lawn underfoot, the stimulating textures of plant foliage, or the feel of soil in their hands. Due to the lack of dress code in our own backyards we tend to go barefoot, enabling us to enjoy the sensation of touch through our feet which is frequently absent from our normal lives. Depending on screening for privacy, and on personal preference, clothes can also be discarded in varying degrees, allowing you to feel the warmth of the sun and the freshness of the breeze on your bare skin. In a resort-style environment, the experiences of touch include the refreshing cool water of a pool or outdoor shower, the massage of a spa's jets, and the comfort of furniture in a dining area or lounge, as well as the soothing heat of its fireplace. Resort-style designs also extend the sensory experience to the way a garden feels, its atmosphere and air of comfort and tranquillity that are so much a part of outdoor living.

GROW

EVERY GARDEN IS DEFINED BY its location, layout and inclusions, but also by the selection and placement of plants. The plants in a garden play a major role in creating its atmosphere and communicate so much about its intended use, but they also give us glimpses of personality and lifestyle. The unique characteristics of each garden bring new opportunities for the selection of plants and how they are displayed. For example, a large selection of plant varieties can be mixed throughout the garden areas, creating contrasts of form, foliage, colour and texture, or a few select plant types could be installed in bulk plantings and groups to create a repetitive theme that connects all parts of the garden. The choice is personal and depends on the intended design, but I often combine the two, with a stronger emphasis on the bulk planting approach.

A resort-style garden commonly lends itself to tropical and subtropical plantings, though it is not limited to those themes and should always reflect the architecture of the home. Formal designs can also be integrated with all the elements and functionality of resort-style living. In these gardens, the formal structures will define the planting style and the use of plant shapes and forms. Hedges take a rightful place in formal gardens, reflecting the building structures and the controlled nature of the environment. Hedging can be used to divide the garden into rooms, bringing an element of mystery while providing privacy and seclusion to those areas, and it is excellent for communicating direction. While hedges will require maintenance to keep them in shape, depending on the garden's size and scale, clipping can be limited to every five or six weeks during the growing seasons. Common hedging plants such as box (*Buxus*), mock orange (*Murraya*) or viburnum (*Viburnum*) are just a few choices that respond well to pruning and shaping; while lavender (*Lavandula*), gardenias (*Gardenia*) or camellias (*Camellia*) can be used for slightly more relaxed hedge plantings that still support the formal style.

In the majority of resort-style gardens, plants with a structural appeal provided by strong forms and leaf shapes will complement the dynamic elements of the design, such as the pool, the chimney of the fireplace or the dining area. Foliage and architectural plants that make dramatic statements include cycads, New Zealand Flax (*Phormium*), Bird of Paradise (*Strelitzia*), the giant yucca (*Yucca guatemalensis*) and *Agave attenuata*, which can also be used in a pot as a stunning focal point. The unique form and appearance of bamboo should be explored, as there are many clumping or non-invasive types that can create great effects in the garden, blending well with other foliage plants, as well as provide valuable screening or filtering. In recent years the popularity and availability of flax lilies (*Dianella*) has increased, not only for the form and colour of their foliage and their flowers in spring and summer, but also for their hardiness and low water use; while *Liriope muscari* has become a landscaper's favourite for its hardiness along with its display of lavender-like flowers. I have always loved the colour and form of Grey Star (*Ctenanthe setosa*) with its leaves that are green-grey on top and purple underneath.

Whatever the garden style, however, an important aspect to consider is the level of maintenance required by the planting selection. All gardens will require some maintenance, to ensure they continue to fulfil the purpose they were designed for. Whether general weeding, mulching, pruning or the removal of spent flowerheads, basic maintenance is essential for the long-term successful growth of any garden. Your garden is something to be enjoyed and to be a part of, and looking after it only enhances the rewarding experiences it brings.

143

My clients have also shared the risks that designing a property can bring, especially with the innovation of custom-made pieces, but they have trusted my design judgement as well. In many cases where there was a plan for the building of a new home on the property, I have changed the placement of the proposed house on the site so that it would benefit from greater views, a better street frontage presence, increased sunlight and accessibility to an indoor—outdoor lifestyle, keeping the bigger picture in mind.

May I encourage you to stretch your imagination when considering your garden and explore the opportunities before you. In resort-style living the garden should firstly be a functional space, catering to all your needs, so consider the placement of all elements and how you will interact with them. Convenience need not be limited to the home so include all those items that assist in a better way of living, whether entertaining with family and friends or relaxing on your own. Explore the many ways that pool design can enhance your use of it, and allow water features to surround the home or even flow through it. Discover the wonder of plants that will bring the total concept alive, adding layers of colour and texture, as well as expressing the intentions of the design, forming a connection between you and your environment. Indulge yourself with inclusions that enhance your time outside, such as a shower or spa. Think outside the box when you are planning your garden. Investigate materials and take chances on colours, textures and shapes that are different to what you are used to. Embrace innovation and challenge the standards, ask questions and consider new products and ideas. Take the time to ask 'What if?' or 'Imagine if?'. These words can lead to an amazing garden design loved by many. The choice is yours: think big, dream bigger and embrace a better outdoor living style.

149

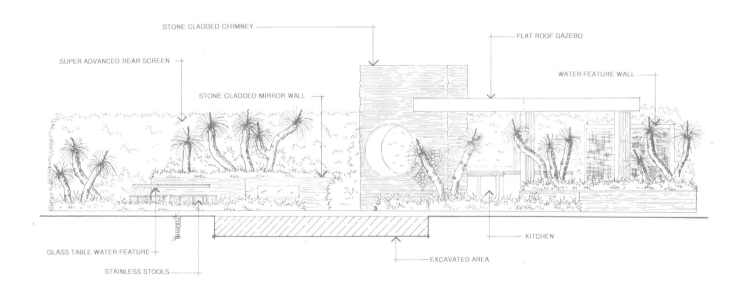

STONE CLADDED CHIMNEY

FLAT ROOF GAZEBO

SUPER ADVANCED REAR SCREEN

WATER FEATURE WALL

STONE CLADDED MIRROR WALL

GLASS TABLE WATER FEATURE

KITCHEN

STAINLESS STOOLS

EXCAVATED AREA

mm

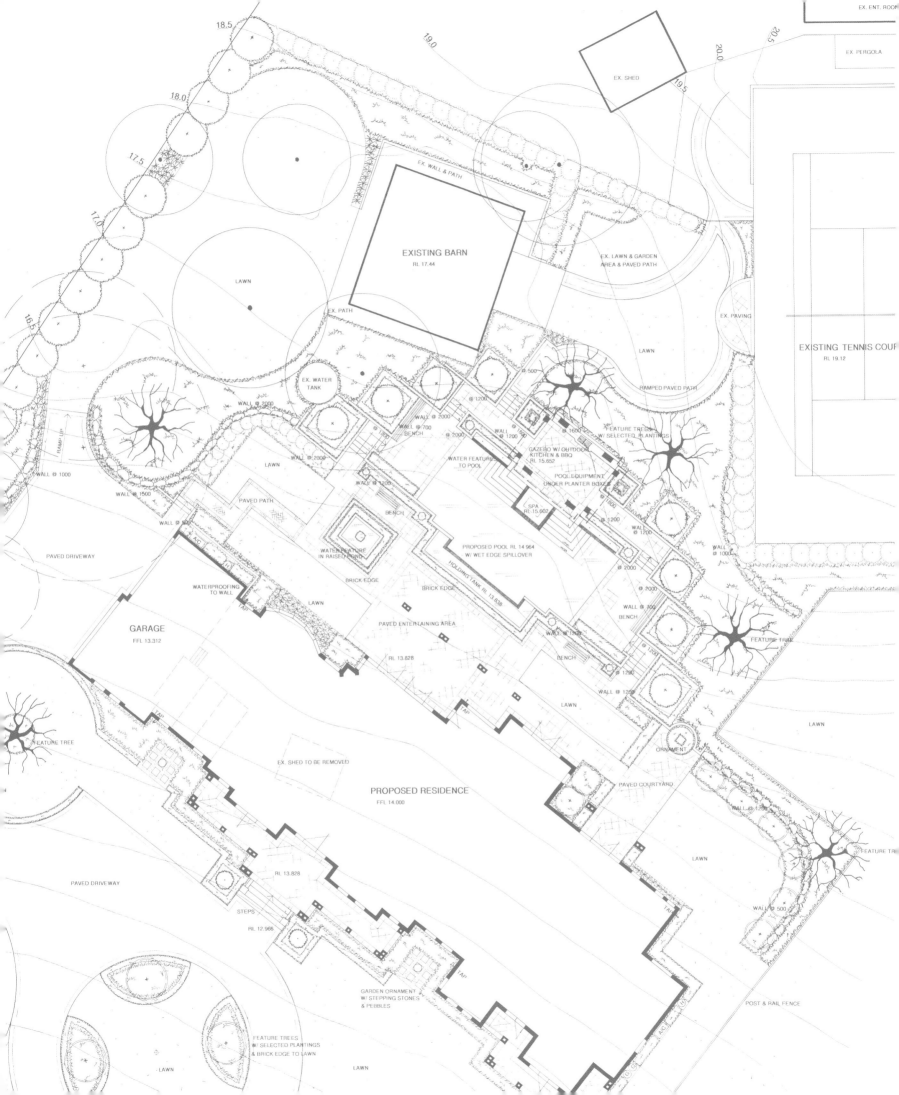

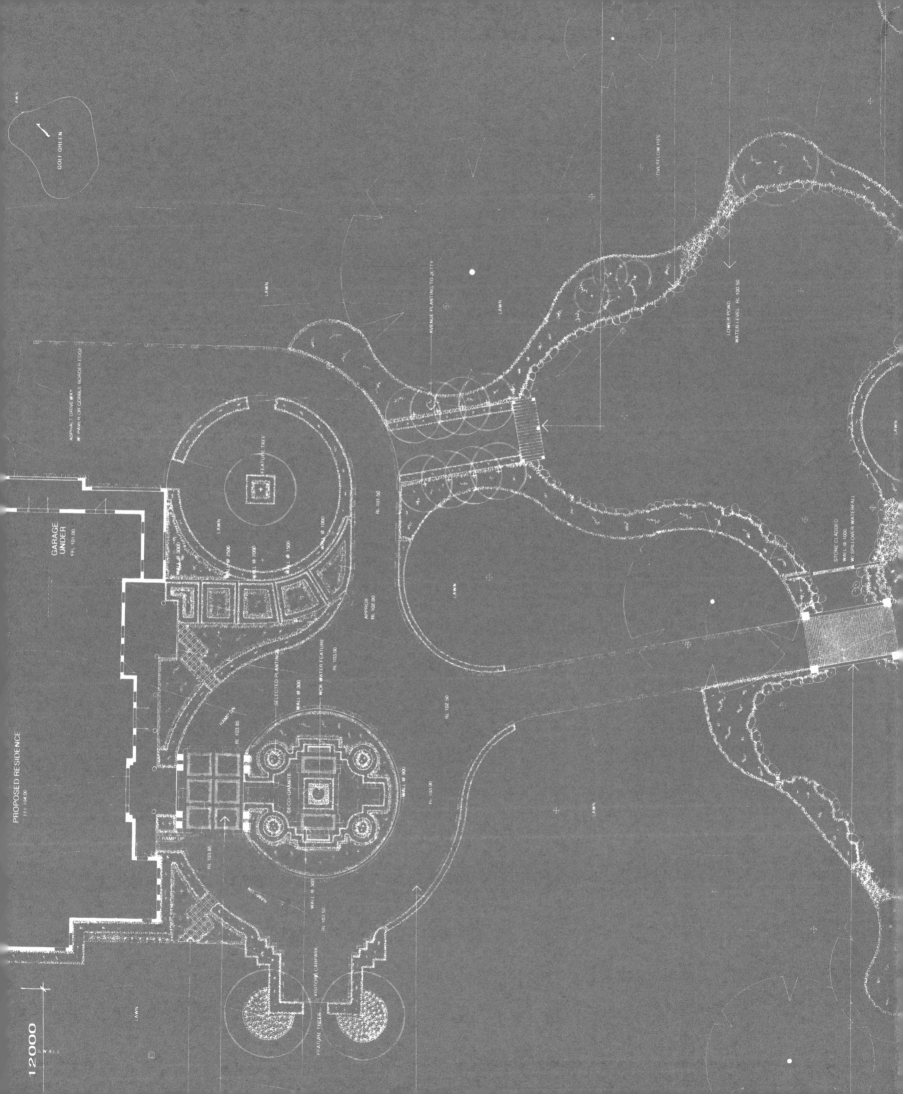